400
H9
1971

THE DECLINE AND FALL
OF RADICAL CATHOLICISM

THE DECLINE AND FALL
OF RADICAL CATHOLICISM

JAMES HITCHCOCK

HERDER AND HERDER

1971
HERDER AND HERDER NEW YORK
232 Madison Avenue, New York 10016

Library of Congress Catalog Card Number: 73-146297
© 1971 by Herder and Herder, Inc.
Manufactured in the United States

Contents

In Memory of
JOHN P. MCKENNA
1935–1970
Tu vero contristabiris sed tristitia tua convertetur in gaudium

Preface

THIS is a book which the author can sincerely say he wishes did not have to be written. Its appearance is one token of the failure of the great hopes for reform which swept through the Church less than a decade ago. There are many kinds of disillusionment in the post-conciliar Church, and this is an attempt to articulate one of them.

Paradoxically, the greatest handicap from which reformers have suffered since the Council is the general absence of reasoned opposition. There has, of course, been no lack of rigid, authoritarian, semi-hysterical polemics on the Right as well as silent, punitive, often covert opposition on the part of bishops and pastors. Such opposition, however, has harmed reformers not only in thwarting their aims but also by confirming them too often in a smug arrogance.

In one sense the book asks the question who is to blame for the failure of reform, and answers that reformers themselves must bear a large share of it. It is not, however, meant to be a sterile *post-mortem* for the sake of pointing a finger, but an attempt to address issues which are still crucial in the Church, and which have not yet been settled.

Moreover, this analysis grows from the inside, not only because the author has lived through the recent changes in the Church, but also because he lays claim himself to the title of progressive which is often severely criticized here. His interest in the reform of the Church dates from his high-school days. He was dismissed as editor of a Catholic college newspaper in a classic censorship dispute (in 1959, before such events attracted wide publicity). He was a participant in the St. John's University faculty strike of 1966, and he is the author of a published exposé of chancery-office machinations in three Midwestern dioceses. He was moderately involved in Eugene McCarthy's presidential campaign and in an effort to evict ROTC from a Catholic university campus. In short, he lays claim to having made his minimum contribution to necessary change and having resisted institutional tyranny, and he lays claim therefore to some right of being heard in criticism.

There is unavoidably some confusion of categories in the book. Although primarily directed at "radicalism," it often does not distinguish this phenomon from "progressivism," "reform," or "liberalism." Although primarily concerned with the American Church, there are occasional strayings elsewhere. Although chiefly interested in Roman Catholicism, there is some use of Protestant sources. The justification for these inconsistencies will probably be obvious to most readers—attitudes which are definably radical are often also shared by those who consider themselves reformists. Problems which afflict American Catholicism are hardly absent among Protestants, Europeans, or Canadians.

No effort has been made here to deal with theology as a formal discipline, or to evaluate theological speculations in a systematic way. Rather the Church has been approached as a living society, and theological ideas have been considered only insofar as they appear to play an important role in the life of that society.

JAMES HITCHCOCK

10

THE DECLINE AND FALL
OF RADICAL CATHOLICISM

1.

The Failure of Reform

In the decade prior to the Second Vatican Council perhaps the most remarkable fact about American Catholic progressives was that they were really conservatives.

In theology the mark of progressivism in those years was dissatisfaction, to a greater or less degree, with the Thomistic theological establishment. The more moderate intellectuals were disciples of Jacques Maritain and Etienne Gilson, who insisted that the Thomism of the colleges and seminaries was a corrupted Thomism, filled with misunderstandings which had crept in during the later Middle Ages and early modern times. Pristine Thomism was considered a much purer and at the same time much more "modern" phenomenon than the common versions shot through with Cartesian or Nominalist errors. To every implication of heresy the reformer could answer proudly that it was his opponents, the establishment itself, who were corrupted by modern errors, while he sought the serene, eternal truth of the Middle Ages.

More daring intellectuals questioned Thomism's usefulness to the modern Catholic. Despite Maritain's insistence that real Thomism was profoundly "existential," these reformers were not convinced and found themselves drawn to the real existentialists, especially the Catholic Gabriel Marcel and the Jewish Martin Buber, but even to the atheist Albert Camus. Yet this

13

earnest reaching out to modernity, this intense desire to experience dread and *Angst* and absurdity in the same way that secular man experienced them, did not indicate loss of traditional faith. On the contrary, Catholic intellectuals of the 1950's were generally convinced that modern existentialism, as a grappling with life, was profoundly in harmony with the spirit of the Bible and the great fathers of the Church, especially the Augustine who had written his *Confessions*. It was rationalism of all kinds, including the rationalism of Thomas Aquinas, which they believed had deformed a Christianity which was really "existential" in its deepest being.

Thus even the Catholic who rejected Thomism was secure from his critics (at least in his own mind) by the thought that while the "orthodox" worshipped a false god created by the Middle Ages, the dissenter was returning to the roots of the faith—personal encounter as the deepest reality, a wrestling with profound human problems, awareness of the paradoxes and absurdities of existence. By coming to grips with modern thought the liberal Catholic believed that he deepened his capacity for "encounter" and thus for a deeper love of God and the mysteries of God revealed through the Church.

Theology inevitably led into liturgy, and one of the surest marks of the Catholic liberal was his interest in the liturgical movement. For some this meant especially the translation of much, but not all, of the Mass into the vernacular. However, vernacularists by no means dominated the movement, and many liberal Catholics believed that the vernacular was unnecessary so long as people were taught to use their missals and to make the Latin responses at the dialogue Mass.

Generally, liturgical progressives were not interested in innovations, in making the Mass more "modern." They were rather concerned about recovering the spirit and reality of the original Mass, before the dubious pieties of the later Middle Ages and the floridities of the Baroque era had disfigured it. Those who resisted liturgical reform could justly be accused of idolatry towards innovations which had crept in many centuries after the Mass in its classic outline had been established. The reformers, far from being innovators who tampered with the sacred drama, were actually purifiers whose battle cry was always "retreat" into the elemental, pre-modern world of simple emotions, agrarian imagery, and sacramental nature. They asked conservatives why they needed grandiose rococo flourishes like lace vestments, clouds of incense, coloratura soloists, and imported marble altars. Did they not believe that when *"Hoc est enim Corpus meum"* was pronounced Christ was really made present? The reformers prided themselves on their fundamentalism with respect to such doctrines: they at least could rest with a naked faith.

Liturgical backwardness was a major cause of the liberal Catholic's dissatisfaction with parish life, although he rarely opted out of the parish. Characteristically, what most distressed him in his parish was the fact that it was too modern, in the bad sense, and too American. There was a pervasive booster spirit —bingo games, Cub Scouts, beer-and-pretzel Holy Name societies, building-fund drives, talk about "parish plants," Sunday Mass rushed through irreverently to alleviate the parking problem, sports idioms used in sermons, and so on.

The sensitive Catholic of the 1950's solaced himself, however, by noting that the parish was not the real Church, precisely because it seemed to have so little to do with traditional Catholic piety of the best kind. Periodic trips to Benedictine or Trappist monasteries refreshed the unhappy progressive and gave him glimpses of true Catholicism, which was like true liturgy in being archaic (but not outdated), beautifully simple, and agrarian. The precious heritage of the High Middle Ages and earlier was still alive and cast its gentle but devastating light on the modern vulgarities which had choked off real Catholic life in the parishes.

The third great area of liberal dissatisfaction in the preconciliar era was political and social. The liberal Catholic often found himself bitterly condemned for his support of the welfare state, his tactical alliances with secular liberals, his repudiation of fanatic anti-Communism, his internationalism, and so on. Here, however, the progressive could play his trump card, for he actually based his political and social opinions squarely on the great papal encyclicals of 1891 and 1931. With some exceptions, Catholic liberals of the Eisenhower era believed that at one time or another the great modern popes had comprehensively pronounced on every important social problem and all that was wanting was for Catholics to implement these teachings.

Thus while the liberal himself was troubled by certain papal actions, such as Pius XII's condemnation of the leading modern philosophies in *Humani Generis* (1950), in general he considered himself a firm papalist and argued that the failures of his conservative brethren were caused by their hyper-Americanism, their deep imbibing of certain forms of nineteenth-century *laissez-faire* liberalism, and their willful ignorance of the sound teachings of the Holy Father. It was a commonplace for liberals of the 1950's to complain that Rome was far ahead of the American bishops on most questions, and it was often implied

16

that greater loyalty to the pope would cure the American Church's worst problems.

In general Catholic liberals before Vatican II could argue their own orthodoxy very convincingly, yet their conservative critics perversely accused them of the worst motivation and, in effect, of dishonesty in explaining their positions.

In theology the conservative insisted that Thomism and orthodox belief were so closely wedded that it was impossible to divorce them without grave consequences. The dissenting intellectuals were suspected of assaulting the outer bastions of Scholastic terminology with an eye eventually to seizing the inner citadel of beliefs like the Trinity, the Resurrection, the Virgin Birth, the Real Presence, and papal infallibility. The progressive insisted that he merely wished to pour old wine into new bottles.

Conservatives were especially concerned over the proposals for liturgical reform. Little there could be faulted on orthodox grounds, but why did the liberals feel this compelling need to tamper with sacred actions centuries old, which had given so much comfort to so many believers and were so dignified and impressive even to the non-believer? In typical hysterical fashion conservative critics charged that if the Church made the least concession, let down the least barricade, the reformers would prove insatiable. Nothing would be treated with respect and sacred awe but would be shunted around at the whim of the liturgist. Conservatives also raised the faith question: If the liberals actually believed in the efficacy of the sacraments, why did they feel a need to reform them?

Somewhat embarrassedly, conservatives countered the triumphant papalism of the political liberals by questioning their sincerity. They charged that the latter did not really love and respect the pope but merely invoked his authority because it was convenient. They insisted, against all reason, that the liberals did not really derive their social principles from Catholic tradition but were actually breathing in the secular humanist air, which they attempted to give a superficial Catholic odor. They were even said to be secretly sympathetic to Marxism, although unwilling to admit this fact publicly.

There were other, less crucial liberal-conservative conflicts before Vatican II which were nonetheless archetypal of what was to come. Liberals were usually ecumenically minded, which did not mean that they were prepared to begin serious theological discussions with Protestants, much less to hold services with them, but that they thought it necessary to concede sincerity and a measure of truth to non-Catholic denominations, to admit many Roman errors at the time of the Reformation, and to be friendly with Protestants in the hope that serious dialogue could one day begin. The conservative believed that ecumenists were interested in other faiths because they were shaky in their own and that the beginning of the "dialogue" would result inevitably in the liberals conceding many fundamental points of Catholic belief.

Liberals also decried Catholic ghettoism with respect to the larger world. They advocated loosening up the curricula of Catholic colleges to allow secular philosophies to be taught non-polemically, more Catholic students and better Newman clubs on secular campuses, and seminaries located near universities so that future priests could encounter "the world" and receive genuine education as opposed to indoctrination. Conservatives were shocked at these proposals and warned that they would result in wholesale abandonment of belief on the part of the students. Liberals countered, as they did to the charges against their ecumenism, that they welcomed the opportunity to test their faith in alien environments, and that they suspected the conservatives of having secret doubts about their own beliefs which they projected onto others.

Despite the fact that the conservative analysis of pre-conciliar Catholic progressivism was often mean-spirited and fanatical, and that it often ignored logic and apparent plain evidence to postulate hidden realities, the conservatives were correct in virtually every particular of their criticism of reform and their predictions of the effects it would have in the Church.

There are still many progressives in the Church of the pre-conciliar kind who want essentially the limited and conservative reform which was then advocated. However, the fulcrum of discussion has shifted sharply leftward in the past few years and the great issues in the Church are now precisely those things which the conservatives once hysterically predicted and liberals emphatically denied. Thomism has disappeared almost without a trace, and there is now scarcely a single traditional doctrine of the Church which is not seriously questioned by some prominent theologians, not excluding the "existence" of God. For many progressives the reform of the liturgy proved merely that the liturgy did indeed, as the conservatives charged, have no meaning for them, and they are now in the process of devising liturgies which have almost no organic connection with those of the Church, or else are abandoning liturgy altogether. They no longer believe it is anything beyond a human invention expressing human needs, and the elimination of the theatrical aura of mystery has effectively eliminated for them belief in the

Real Presence as well. Advanced Catholics now have little patience with the social teachings of the Church, are frankly and militantly secular in their concerns, and would like to strip the pope of his powers. The encounter with Protestants in ecumenical dialogue and with humanists on the secular campus has indeed led to a wholesale abandonment of vast amounts of Catholic belief and tradition, and many of the avant-garde now wonder if anything in the Church is worth saving.

Ecumenism is perhaps the best index of how far radical Catholics have travelled in a few years' time. John O'Connor, a lay journalist, admits that it is often easier to love Protestants than one's fellow Catholics,[1] and the liturgist Father Gerard Sloyan believes that the Anglican Church is actually more apostolic than the Roman Church.[2] Attending a Catholic theological conference in Europe the American Baptist Langdon Gilkey found little he could disagree with,[3] and another American Protestant, John C. Bennett, finds Catholics taking the sacraments less seriously.[4] Robert McAfee Brown, a Presbyterian theologian, has remarked that "so much water has gone over the theological dam, and so much dogmatic debris has followed the same route."[5] (The ease with which cherished traditions have become debris is one of the more inhumane aspects of reform.) Some radical Protestant ecumenists have carried little baggage of any kind, dross or gold, and it seems clear that Catholics have given up far more than have Protestants. It would be difficult, in fact, to think of a single important way in which Protestants have become more Catholic in the post-conciliar period, and Catholic radicals have gotten along best with Protestant ecumenists who show little respect for or understanding of Catholic traditions.

20

Thus Baptist theologian Harvey Cox attends a conference at St. Peter's at the Pope's invitation and muses that before long the building will be merely another monument to a dead faith. Elsewhere he suggests that monasteries be turned into retreat and conference centers.[6] (Despite his great influence in Catholic circles, Cox shows perhaps less ability to appreciate Catholicism than any other leading ecumenist.) Anglican Bishop John Robinson, author of *Honest to God,* smugly congratulates himself on the fact that many Catholic laymen confide things to him that they would never tell their own bishops.[7] Arthur Crabtree, a Protestant theologian at a Catholic university, asks in an ecumenical journal whether the pope is Antichrist. He acquits John XXIII of the charge but avoids mentioning whether it applies to his predecessors or successor.[8] Everett Gendler, a liberal rabbi, includes references to Jesus in Jewish services but warns that Christians must abandon belief in "Jesus . . . as supernatural purger of sin" in favor of "involved sufferer on behalf of fellow men. . . . This makes the Cross not a static institutional dogma but a living symbol."[9]

The radical Catholic's ecumenical harmony with the secular world is also bought at the expense of everything authentically Catholic. The radicals have affirmed the value of secularity and the holiness of secular man, but secular man has not reciprocated towards the Church. Frederick Franck, a Dutch journalist of no denomination, offers the Church a model for the ideal pope which is scarcely distinguishable from the ideal United Nations secretary general. Such a pope must, of course, first overcome "the anti-evangelical mode of existence of all institutional religions . . ."[10] The French Communist Roger Garaudy has proven the independence of his thought by his expulsion from the central committee of the Party. But his *rapprochement* with Christianity seems to involve the virtual denial of the core traditions of faith: the man called Christ, whose true name is unknown, came to show man that a wholly new beginning in life can be made at any moment. He was crucified for preaching against the Establishment and leading an uprising of the poor.[11] (This is certainly more Marx than St. Paul.) Lay theologian Rosemary Ruether warns that no dialogue with Marxism is possible from the standpoint of "Constantinian Christianity" (which seems to mean the main body of the Church for the past 1600 years). Only by recovering the left-wing sectarian perspective can Christians hope that Marxists will take them seriously.[12] Whatever intrinsic value these ideas may have, there is nothing ecumenical about them; they involve the wholesale surrender of one side to the other.

In the conciliar years, conservatives charged that reform was really the "Protestantizing" of the Church, and radical Catholicism since the Council has been precisely a wholesale adoption of classic Protestant attitudes. Not only is papal authority repudiated, but often episcopal and priestly authority as well, and insofar as radicals have a theory of church organization it appears to be close to Congregationalism. As in classic Protestantism, tradition is conceded no authority and little respect; there is a pervasive biblicism, although some more daring radicals are moving beyond the Bible also. The Eucharist is regarded as at best a symbolic act, in the classic Zwinglian sense, or as a community meal; there is no mystical reality present. The other sacraments, except marginally baptism, are largely ignored, thus in effect denying them as the Reformers did 400 years ago.

22

Radical Catholic theology derives little from Catholic or Orthodox traditions and much from Protestant thought of the past
150 years, especially German. Distinctive Catholic devotions and
practices have been entirely abandoned in most avant-garde
circles.

The miraculous ecumenical unity achieved by the radicals in
the past few years is therefore quite easy to account for—as
reactionaries predicted, the most advanced Catholics simply became Protestants, except in name. Their ecumenism is now
revealed to have been motivated precisely by serious inner
doubts about Catholicism. This wholesale conversion can be
superficially denied both because the radicals often continue to
call themselves Catholics and because they usually unite with
Protestant radicals who are often severely critical of their own
churches. However, as Lutheran historian Martin Marty has
pointed out, the "Protestant principle" is not a critique of the
Church from the outside but rather a recalling of the group to
its own unique reality.[13] Radical Protestants, in their self-criti-
cisms, are merely calling on their churches to venture further
in classic Protestant directions. Catholic radicals, however, are
quite precisely calling for the Roman Church to follow the same
directions which Protestantism has chosen. They are asking that
the historic Catholic Church simply cease to exist and that
Catholics join in a common form of radical Protestantism.

No one can love or respect someone else unless he first loves
and respects himself. This may be a truism, but it is precisely
healthy self-love which radical Catholics have often lacked in
their approaches to other religions and to the secular world.
They saw their partners in dialogue as agents of liberation from

23

their own pasts; they learned a great deal but taught little. No unanimity, no community, built on such a basis can possibly endure.

There are many curiosities in the history of the Church in the post-conciliar years, and not the least is the fact that so few progressives have noticed the extent to which the reactionaries' predictions prior to the Council have been proven correct and that their own expectations have been contradicted. They continue to treat the conservatives as ignorant, prejudiced, and out of touch with reality.

Yet the progressives' hope for "renewal" now seems largely chimeric, a grandiose expectation, an attractive theory, but one which has failed of achievement. In the heady days of the Council it was common to hear predictions that the conciliar reforms would lead to a massive resurgence of the flagging Catholic spirit. Laymen would be stirred from their apathy and alienation and would join enthusiastically in apostolic projects. Liturgy and theology, having been brought to life and made relevant, would be constant sources of inspiration to the faithful. The religious orders, reformed to bring them into line with modernity, would find themselves overwhelmed with candidates who were generous and enthusiastic. The Church would find the number of converts increasing dramatically as it cast off its moribund visage and indeed would come to be respected and influential in worldly circles as it had not been for centuries. In virtually every case the precise opposite of these predictions has come to pass.

This is not to say that important reforms have not been successfully implemented in the Church, that new visions of what it means to be a Catholic have not opened, and that for

24

many persons the reformed Church is not an immeasurably freer place than it ever was. Fundamentally, however, in terms of the all-pervading spiritual revival which was expected to take place, renewal has obviously been a failure. Virtually everyone in the Church is now more uneasy, more suspicious, more apprehensive than before the Council. More people are now totally alienated, both on the Left and on the Right. Little in the Church seems entirely healthy or promising; everything seems vaguely sick and vaguely hollow. No one can predict with any certainty that the Church will have a visible existence by the end of the century.

In their refusal to consider seriously their own failures and miscalculations, many reformist Catholics have taken refuge in the idea that the Council itself somehow failed. According to a common radical myth, the Council raised enormous expectations for change, but its decrees either fell short of what was truly desired or else were never adequately implemented. The bitterness and demoralization prevalent among so many Catholics is thus explained by the fact that their hopes were raised and then rudely dashed.

Such a theory shows how far many radicals now go in repudiating the past, even their own recent past. In fact, Vatican II exceeded the hopes of the liberals, and the changes which have already been implemented in the Church are so extensive that ten years ago they would have been unthinkable. As Michael Novak wrote in 1965, "few of us nine or ten years ago foresaw that a Council would soon realize many of our dreams; we expected to battle another generation or two before having won so much." [14]

On the eve of the Council in 1962, *Commonweal* published

a series of articles by some of the most prominent American Catholic intellectuals and reformers, detailing their hopes for the coming assembly. There was not a single suggestion which might be called radical. Most concentrated on such modest issues as a partially vernacular liturgy, a greater role for the laity in the parishes, and the collegiality of the bishops. One commentator raised the birth-control issue but hastened to add that he was not questioning the teaching and suggested that the problem was that rhythm was presented in too negative a light.[15] The lay magazine *Jubilee* also published its readers' opinions as to what the Council ought to accomplish. A few persons mentioned tentatively the question of remarriage after divorce. Birth control was mentioned fairly often, but otherwise there was no proposal which was even remotely radical.[16]

There is no question, then, that Vatican II initiated almost every major reform which American progressives, prior to 1965, generally desired. It is true, of course, that many of those in authority remained unsympathetic to these reforms and tried, with varying degrees of success, to impede them. But remarkable progress has been made nonetheless. Birth control, which the most ardent progressives discussed only very tentatively in the pre-conciliar years, was the major problem not touched by the Council. Yet even here few laymen could now claim to be oppressed by this teaching, since they widely ignore it. There is no honest way of calling the Council a failure.

How then can the bitterness, the disappointment, the deep disillusionment of post-conciliar American progressives be explained? Daniel Callahan, perhaps the most influential American layman of the decade, saw the answer: "The faster the change, the faster they [the progressives] raise their sights: any slowdown, any obstacle, brings on a quick state of funk. At the same time it is turning out that a new liturgy, a new theology, a new biblical exegesis, a new collegiality, don't necessarily produce the kind of rejuvenation everyone thought they would. That unexpected revelation has driven many back to far more basic issues: God, belief, the meaning (if any) of Christ himself." [17]

This insight has, quite remarkably, not achieved very wide currency in progressive circles. The official progressive myth continues to argue that it was not the reformers discovering the inadequacy of their own ideas and programs which brought disillusionment but rather the institutional Church, which refused calls for meaningful reform. In the post-conciliar years the progressives have become increasingly radical and also increasingly paranoid. They manifest an extreme reluctance to examine honestly their own attitudes and their own history and a corresponding compulsion to blame all failures on "the establishment."

To change one's mind, especially in a period of great turmoil and uncertainty, is no dishonor, and the post-conciliar Catholic radicals can of course argue that they simply underestimated the task of reform. However, such an excuse is too easy, since it frees the radical from the necessity of coming to terms with his own past, of asking forgiveness for his own sins, of assuming his share of blame for failure. Here as elsewhere the radical often presents himself as an almost passive creature of history, not really responsible for his opinions, since they are merely formed by the changing times.

The emergence of radical Catholicism cannot be explained as simply the desire to push beyond the reforms of the Council, as the logical and inevitable extension of earlier and more moderate attitudes. The radicals implicitly repudiate the earlier reform movement as much as they repudiate the conservatives. They are not simply extending the moderate reform but are moving in new and totally alien directions, and in many cases specifically negating much that was central to the spirit of conciliar reform.

An instructive example of this movement is the theological odyssey of Daniel Callahan himself, which could be a paradigm for the development of many less celebrated laymen during the decade of reform. In 1960 Mr. Callahan was attacked by a Dominican priest who demanded that Catholic intellectuals demonstrate their acceptance of "transcendental Christianity." Replying with the patience which in those days was characteristic of reformers, Mr. Callahan denied that such assurance was necessary and warned his critic not to assume the worst.[18] By 1965, however, he seemed to be endorsing Harvey Cox's proposal that Christians should forget about "God-ideas" and should busy themselves with "liberating the captives." By the following year he was writing, with considerable assurance, that "I do not find anything in my present experience that I am tempted to call 'transcendental,'" and ". . . some Christians today find action more meaningful for them than contemplation, the experience of human solidarity more binding than an insight into the being of God . . . man's making over the earth more electrifying than theistic accounts of the way God sustains all being."[19]

In 1962 the Apostolic Delegate to the United States gave an address at Marquette University in which he questioned the loyalty and orthodoxy of Catholic intellectuals. There was an understandable uproar, and afterwards Mr. Callahan was among those signing a letter in which it was denied that intellectuals "are of a set purpose compromising traditional Catholic positions." [20] A few weeks later he spoke loyally of "the authority of the Church, or its divinely ordained means of teaching and preserving the deposit of faith." [21] The next year he wrote, in answer to the charge that progressive laymen sought to overthrow "the hierarchical, authoritarian structure of the Church," that "there is no evidence to support such an assertion." [22] By 1966, however, he was insisting that not even "elements central to the core meaning of the Bible" should be regarded as beyond question, and that "there can never be any final commitment to the Bible." [23] In the meantime, of course, any vestige of belief in an authoritative church had disappeared from Mr. Callahan's thought. (In 1970 he admitted being bored with the whole subject of Church reform, and he found "conservative Christianity intellectually unsound." [24])

No doubt Mr. Callahan, as other Catholic reformers, was sincere in the assurances he gave his critics concerning his own orthodoxy. Objectively, however, many of the more prominent reformers insisted that they desired reform only in accordance with the traditions and authority of the Church, when in reality within themselves they were already beginning to repudiate almost everything which was part of historic Roman Catholicism. Many doubtful bishops and apprehensive laymen were persuaded to support reform by assurances of the kind Mr. Callahan gave in 1960-1963, only to discover later that those who had urged these reforms were no longer interested in them and even regarded them as meaningless. For a rigid, closed system like the pre-conciliar Church, the most creative and fruitful moment of its development is likely to be the precise instant at which it opens itself, which in recent times has been the immediate conciliar years when reformers enjoyed the benefits of both tradition and innovation. That moment was soon passed, however, leading to an unbalanced and disoriented kind of radicalism tending to degenerate into fanaticism and bitterness.

In the pre-conciliar years many liberal Catholics deluded themselves into believing that their dissatisfactions with seminary Scholasticism, parish life, Baroque liturgy, benighted clergy, and so on were peripheral to real Catholicism, that in fact it was precisely because they were true Catholics that they were offended by the poor copy of the faith which they were offered. By the end of the 1960's, however, many such progressives were forced to realize that their dislike of Scholasticism, their hankering after liturgical reform, their visits to choice monasteries, were really attempts to overcome a gnawing crisis of faith which they either did not recognize, lacking adequate self-knowledge, or did not want to recognize. However uncharitable, their conservative critics were simply right in postulating weakness of fundamental belief as being at the root of many liberals' dissatisfaction.

Yet what should be to the radicals the most embarrassing aspect of their history over the past ten years is their misreading not only of their own intellectual and psychic motions but of the movements of society as well. The progressives prided themselves on their relative worldliness, their sophisticated understanding of secular, social-science realities. Yet the conservatives, burdened with the unempirical Scholastic temperament, foresaw far more clearly than the progressives the realities of change. The progressives blithely assumed a period of swift, painless reform, in which desirable changes could be accomplished while

30

undesirable ones were restrained. The conservatives realized that no large and intricate society like the Catholic Church can be changed without considerable dislocation and outright loss, and they realized also that stated programs for reform are never realized as they are set forth and that change tends to generate change, so that those who begin as moderate reformers sometimes end as revolutionaries. As Daniel Callahan observed, "We were woefully remiss in understanding of social and psychological factors." [25]

The chief dishonesty of the reformers was their studious concealment, even from themselves, of the problem of belief, until almost the end of the decade of reform. Theological language, liturgical forms, vigorous social action, the uses of authority, the styles of Catholic life, all were seen and discussed as problems. But never faith. As late as 1968 the former English priest Charles Davis was chastizing avant-garde Catholics for the evasions they used to avoid the faith problem, for continuing in the Church in some sense without asking themselves what if anything they believed was true about it.[26] Rosemary Ruether also affirmed at the end of the decade that faith was the central issue and said that "Catholic liberals will discover that, in matters of faith, they are like columns of sand held up by external props with very little backbone of their own." [27] (If this remark had been made by a conservative bishop in 1962 there would have been howls of outrage.)

In retrospect it is possible to see the preoccupation of the progressives with changes of various kinds as a way of avoiding the ultimate question of their own faith. The struggle for reform itself gave meaning to Church membership for those who could not find a deeper meaning. Only towards the end of the

31

1960's, as interest in reform finally waned and as significant new reforms seemed unlikely, did the problem of faith finally come to the surface, and many progressives found little fundamental belief on which they could rest.

In 1965 Daniel Callahan had in fact asked, "But is it inconceivable . . . that this cry for relevance masks a weakening sense of the intelligibility, the rationality, the intrinsic plausibility of Christianity in its transtemporal, supernatural meaning?" However, he stressed that he was suggesting this only as a possible hypothesis and not as a likelihood.[28] The same year he also suggested that the private dishonesty of progressives lay in their belief that everything they did was in the service of the Church, when in reality they were perhaps suffering fundamental but unacknowledged doubts.[29] Somehow these insights were never seriously entertained by reformers.

Responsibility for the failure of *aggiornamento* must be about evenly apportioned between rigid reactionaries, especially in the hierarchy, who never believed in reform and did little to implement it, and radical innovators with little commitment to historic Catholicism who nonetheless had a disproportionate influence in the reform movement. Naturally, these two extremes have constantly fed on each other, each serving as a bogey which gives the other a certain credibility.

The radicals have discredited the cause of reform precisely because they have made it appear to be a process of unending strife, instability, and abandonment of cherished beliefs. Many conservatives have a certain justification in believing that the Church was led into a trackless wilderness by guides who then abandoned it because they had lost interest in the journey.

Justified suspicion of radical programs is further reinforced by the suspicion that what motivates the radicals is less their concern for the Church and the majority of its members than their continuing process of self-discovery. They are trying to find themselves, and they wish to use the Church for this purpose. This attitude, directed at personal therapy rather than institutional reform, helps explain the extreme bitterness which characterizes some radicals now. The progressive layman of 1960 was far less unhappy than the progressive layman of 1970, despite the fact that the atmosphere of the Church was earlier much more repressive than it is now, and there was not even realistic hope for change. The increasing bitterness is often caused not by the frustration of hopes for reform but by the radical's discovery that everything which he earnestly thought he wanted has failed to bring him peace. It is the discovery of the empty spaces within himself, rather than the empty spaces in the Church, which is profoundly demoralizing.

Notes

1. *America,* April 9, 1966, p. 484.
2. *National Catholic Reporter,* July 3, 1970, p. 3.
3. *St. Louis Review,* Sept. 23, 1970, p. 6.
4. *National Catholic Reporter,* Oct. 23, 1970, p. 13.
5. *Commonweal,* Nov. 14, 1969, p. 216.
6. *Ibid.,* April 25, 1969, p. 160; and May 1, 1970, p. 160.
7. *The Critic,* Oct.-Nov., 1968, p. 29.
8. *Journal of Ecumenical Studies,* Spring, 1969, pp. 243-4.
9. *New York Times,* March 1, 1970, p. 53.
10. *Commonweal,* Oct. 31, 1969, pp. 164-5.
11. Quoted by John Deedy, *Commonweal,* Feb. 13, 1970, p. 522.
12. *Ibid.,* Jan. 16, 1970, p. 424.
13. *America,* Aug. 31, 1968, p. 123.
14. *Commonweal,* Oct. 8, 1965, p. 12.

15. *Ibid.,* June 8, 1962, p. 276; June 29, 1962, pp. 346-8; July 6, 1962, p. 371; July 13, 1962, pp. 394-6; Aug. 10, 1962, p. 441; Sept. 21, 1962, pp. 511-4; July 27, 1962, pp. 424-5.

16. *Jubilee,* Oct., 1962, pp. 9-19.

17. *Commonweal,* Mar. 3, 1967, p. 622.

18. *Ibid.,* July 8, 1960, p. 349.

19. *Ibid.,* Aug. 19, 1966, pp. 530, 532.

20. *Ibid.,* July 28, 1962, p. 425.

21. *Ibid.,* Aug. 10, 1962, p. 441.

22. Callahan, *The Mind of the Catholic Layman* (New York, 1963), p. 109.

23. *Commonweal,* Dec. 9, 1966, p. 293.

24. *National Catholic Reporter,* Nov. 6, 1970, p. 11.

25. *Commonweal,* Mar. 3, 1967, p. 624.

26. *Ibid.,* Mar. 15, 1968, pp. 715-6.

27. *Ibid.,* Nov. 14, 1969, p. 218.

28. Callahan, *Generation of the Third Eye* (New York, 1965), p. 12.

29. Callahan, *Honesty in the Church* (New York, 1965), pp. 92-7.

2.

Old Priests Writ Large

THE reformer before Vatican II tended to focus his unhappiness on certain attitudes, certain styles of thinking and acting, and to believe that reform of the Church was principally a matter of reforming these attitudes, of somehow purging a mentality which was fundamentally unchristian, and planting instead something both humanly better and at the same time more truly Catholic.

The key word was "charity." Trying themselves to be as charitable as possible, the progressives mounted a systematic critique of the conservatives which showed, without great difficulty, that the latter were quite often nasty, vindictive people whose professed Christianity was an embarrassment, since it so obviously ignored the gentleness of Christ and the traditional importance of fraternal charity within the Church. Most seriously this involved authoritarianism—the willing use of naked coercion and dictatorial methods to insure orthodoxy. It countenanced dishonesty, in which scandals were suppressed and Catholics were systematically protected from alien ideas. Meanness and vituperativeness were not uncommon (as exemplified especially by Father Richard Ginder of *Our Sunday Visitor*), and the very existence of liberal Catholicism was usually declared illegitimate. Progressives, on the other hand, generally advocated a more sparing use of authority (especially withholding it from political affairs and the intellectual life), open and charitable discussion, and self-criticism within the Church.

This vision of the "open Church" which dominated liberal thinking before the Council has come no closer to realization than most of the other dreams of renewal. Here again the most ardent reformers are inclined to blame principally the authorities, or the masses, without considering seriously how much they have themselves contributed to the death of an ideal.

The ideal of fraternal charity was perhaps the first to disappear among reformers, not only in practice but even in theory. It ceased to be regarded as even desirable and was seen by the purer spirits as a sign of weakness and lack of commitment to change. In 1962 the editor of *Commonweal*, James O'Gara, wrote that criticism "must not be bitter; it must be based on love and loyalty to the Church. If it is anything else it is worthless." [1] Daniel Callahan, writing about the conservative layman Garry Wills, was disturbed by Wills' two minds—one scholarly, the other "polemical, cutting, downright unpleasant at times." [2] A year later Callahan warned gently that a bad tone—sometimes bitter and mean—was entering the liberals' writings. [3]

Yet as early as 1966 the very idea of charitable dialogue had been rejected by John O'Connor, who had become a liberal hero after he was ousted as editor of the Wilmington, Delaware, diocesan paper. "It is fantastically naïve," he wrote, "to hold that some kind of Marquis of Queensbury rules can be agreed on to control discussion of the public affairs of the Church." [4]

The implication of Mr. O'Connor's pronouncement seemed to be that hitting below the belt was now permissible among Catholic polemicists, and this soon became almost routine. There is no way by which conservative spokesmen of the 1950's can be distinguished from radical spokesmen of the 1960's on the basis of charity, rationality, open-mindedness, or respect for their opponents. Thus the Trappist theologian Anselm Atkins characterizes the ordinary pious Catholic as a "superstitious religious caterpillar." [5] Rosemary Ruether, not content with disagreeing with the pope over *Humanae Vitae,* now says that he ". . . lie(s) to the whole world to justify his own infallibility . . ." [6] In some radical circles the vehemence of one's feelings against the hierarchy is taken as an index of genuine Christianity. The climax of radical mean-spiritedness came at the 1969 meeting of the American bishops, where the vice-president of the National Association of Laymen, Don Nicodemus, obtained a conference with three bishops and then insulted them with the most obscene epithet imaginable.[7] (An apology was eventually issued by the organization and by Nicodemus, who later resigned.)

Certain radical spokesmen were generally free from vituperativeness. However, following Mr. Callahan's gentle warning of 1965, few of the saner radicals saw any need to dissociate themselves from the mounting swell of irresponsible bitterness and vindictiveness which began to characterize the Catholic Left. Neither did they make any visible efforts to moderate the swell. On the whole, it is also quite dubious whether the Catholic reform movement after Vatican II has been more honest or more open that the established Church it has undertaken to criticize. Indeed, in his influential book *Honesty in the Church,* Mr. Callahan criticized "that form of honesty . . . which is drawn to exposés, to brutal revelations, to battering human feelings (especially of those in authority) in the name of frankness and candor. The great advantage of honesty as a weapon of destruction is that no one can argue against it without at the same time seeming to approve deception." [8]

During the earlier 1960's, when the inside-front cover of *Commonweal* was the responsibility of John Leo, some effort was made to catalogue the follies and vices of the progressives as well as of the establishment. Later, as the page came under the direction of John Deedy, it became a virtually unrelieved summary of machinations in high places, with virtually never a mention of reformist excesses, as though such did not exist. This shift was part of a shift in *Commonweal* itself, and in great part of the Catholic Left, in which significant self-criticism became virtually non-existent and a continuing tone of jeering, demoralizing contempt prevailed. (In 1969 Mr. Leo, no longer with the magazine, advised the editors to pay no attention to those who urged a more reasonable tone, observing that "nobody thinks that way any more.") [9]

In both religious and secular politics the key word by the late 1960's was "polarization," and within the Church the contending sides not only found it difficult and finally impossible to communicate with or respect each oher, but on the Left at least there developed a conscious effort to increase this chasm of division, to deny systematically even the possibility of reconciliation or compromise. The lay theologian Mary Daly thus wrote that "Some have tried to find a way out by employing a weak notion of 'balance,' of 'following a middle road'—which may be an escape for the timid, but hardly profound or satisfying." [10] John Deedy charged that the National Federation of Priests' Councils had been "coopted" by the bishops and cited as his major evidence the Federation president's statement that the organization was centrist and not extremist.[11] John O'Connor characterized "balance" as "a favorite word among the timid" [12] and insisted that "the leadership can't be in the middle." [13] The Jesuit sociologist Norbert Rigali thought it was a dubious assumption that compromises between conservatives and liberals within religious orders were either possible or desirable.[14] The radicals gain adherents in proportion as they convince moderates that it is necessary to choose between the Holy Office and the underground Church. Incidents such as Mr. Nicodemus's insulting of the bishops begin to appear calculated rather than impulsive; the radical stance would be badly undercut if meaningful dialogue between the bishops and their critics could be established.

By the end of the 1960's the movement for radical change within the Church had become a collection of pressure groups, loosely structured and decentralized, but nonetheless aimed at realizing certain goals by political tactics. This was acknowledged, even with pride, by many radicals, who had suddenly awakened into a worldly sophistication and scorned their idle youthful dreams about charity and renewal.

Politics has always been important in the Church, and there is no reason why reformers should not be as political as the established authorities. The politicization of Catholic radicalism continues to exist, however, with a self-conception by which the radical often sees himself as one of the true followers of Jesus. The radical ignores the fact that by becoming political, by searching out methods of pressure and power, he is forced to adopt many of the stances and attitudes of the hierarchy which he formerly condemned as unchristian. The virtual disappearance of radical

39

self-criticism, the open contempt towards those who disagree, the denial even of the possibility of reconciliation within the Church, are all made necessary by the radical's awareness that he does belong to a political group and that it is folly for such a group to concede even the slightest advantage to its opponents. Thus dishonesty becomes endemic and necessary for the radical as well as for the conservative.

The first of these dishonesties concerns the reality of power itself. James O'Gara said in 1961 that "the kind of laymen I have in mind has no desire to take over the priestly role" and that "his views do not reflect any radical or rebellious impulse on his part." [15] Editorializing on a Baltimore lay synod the following year, *Commonweal* said, "The worst possible outcome would be to conceive of the laity as a potentially strong pressure group, in need only of guidance to make them a fearsome political power." [16] The same year, Mr. O'Gara denied that real anti-clericalism existed in the American Church and called anti-clericalism "a deadly virus which can be fatal to Catholic life. It involves a denial of the special role of the ordained priest and the central role of the hierarchy. I do not see how anyone can be anti-clerical in this fundamental sense and remain a Catholic . . ." [17] In 1965 Michael Novak wrote that "Laymen do not seek power, only responsibility." [18] Donald Thorman, later to serve as publisher of *The National Catholic Reporter* (perhaps the most influential of all liberal Catholic publications), wrote a celebrated book in which he insisted that even the frankest and most controversial laymen were "thoroughly loyal to Christ and His Church *and* obedient to [their] religious superiors." [19]

Certainly, none of the reformers who gave these earnest

assurances intended to mislead their readers, but they played nonetheless a dubious role by preparing the way for the politicized radicalism of the later 1960's, in which picketing, sit-ins, organized pressure groups, threatened priests' strikes, withholding of contributions, and so on, were all seen as quite legitimate weapons and in which it was a mark of naïveté to believe that reform could be achieved by any means other than coercion. The moderates who decried such attitudes a few years earlier were now silent. It was in *Commonweal,* still edited by Mr. O'Gara, that in 1969 Mary Daly proposed that since the concept of priesthood is closely related to the notion of the sacred, which is itself rapidly disappearing, the name and reality of the priesthood should simply be abandoned in the Church.[20] The fact that many priests are linked with this anticlericalism does not alter the fact, since these are priests who wear their status lightly, who see no significant distinction between themselves and their lay associates, and who are often in the process of leaving the established priesthood.

Radical Catholics who are determined to be realistic and political should acknowledge that their struggle, like all political struggles, is only in part for the high Christian and human ideals which they profess. All political struggles soon come to be contests over power for its own sake. Most such struggles are also status conflicts, and historians of the future are likely to suggest that in part at least the present upheaval in the Church is a bid by restless, ambitious, talented, and articulate laymen to strip the clergy of their entrenched authority.

The power of the ecclesiastical establishment is on the whole much greater than any power the dissidents can muster, but this does not mean that the dissidents are powerless, as they

41

sometimes present themselves. The threat of massive defections from the Church has been a major inhibiting force on the hierarchy and has caused them to moderate their authority in many instances. Dissidents have also discovered that there is very little which bishops can actually do to a radical layman.

The radicals' most important weapon, however, has been publicity, and they quite early learned its great potential and how to exploit it. By nature a closed, rigid structure like the Catholic hierarchy shuns bad publicity and will often permit considerable deviant activity under its jurisdiction rather than suffer a sensational exposé.

Radical Catholics have thus often found themselves playing for headlines as a means of frightening those in authority. This is a process which is not invalid, especially in a democracy, but it is a process whereby a premium is placed on dramatic, highly simplified, emotional "news," and of necessity a good part of the truth in a given situation is obscured, distorted, or deliberately suppressed. Playing for headlines, which has been the deliberate aim of many radical organizations and individuals, serves a good purpose when it brings patent injustices to public notice and reverses them. The press is almost wholly incapable, however, of dealing with the properly religious dimensions of the Church—theology, spirituality, personal religious experience—and radicals have caused these things to be irretrievably cheapened through the vulgarized treatment they have often gained for them in the headlines. Thomas Merton, himself something of a radical, said that ". . . publicity confuses the issue by the vulgarity, the triviality, the lack of perspective and the ultimate deadening mediocrity by which it turns everything it touches to dust and ashes." [21] James Kavanaugh, a former priest who created a considerable sensation by his writings, was franker than most radicals in acknowledging what he was doing. "I'm working on the modern magisterium, public opinion," he wrote.[22]

The conflicts within the post-conciliar Church for a while stimulated a great popular interest in religious news, which the press duly fed. Just as quickly this sensationalism caused many people to become heartily sick of religion, and the ultimate result was the disillusionment of a large number of people who might otherwise have responded to the new religious movements of the age. It was a high price which many radicals were willing to pay in their power struggles with the establishment.

It is of crucial importance to ask whether a victory by the radicals would in fact lead to a Church more open, more honest, less authoritarian, and more humane that at present. The character of most American bishops makes it difficult to doubt this fact. But it is also impossible to have effective revolution, which is what the radicals desire, without having authoritarianism, strong discipline, enforced orthodoxy, the sacrifice of individuals to the cause—all the abuses which revolutionaries object to in the establishment. These signs have already begun to appear within radical American Catholicism.

Catholic liberals before the Council professed to object to all forms of fanaticism. They regarded the methods of proselytizing often used in the Church as vulgar and inhumane—high-pressure tactics not commensurate with the spirit of the Gospel. They deplored the tendency to divide the world into "us" and "them," the saved and the damned, those with the truth versus those who were ignorant. They questioned, in fact, the very idea of conversion, except for those who came forward

43

voluntarily. Yet by the end of the decade many of these same reformers had been "radicalized," which meant that they now approved the spirit of fanaticism, that proselytizing was an essential, that the world was once again divided between "us" and "them," although the distinction was now basically political. Thus Francis Carling, a Catholic student radical, denounces the fanaticism and bigotry to which he was exposed in the Catholic schools, but is also capable of writing, "The personalism of the student New Left . . . is the only philosophy of politics which does not call for the destruction of all other political philosophies but merely for their reform," [23] an absurdity of which only the true believer could be capable.

The neo-fanaticism of the late 1960's perhaps indicated the religious radical's unusual sensitivity to the needs of the poor and the blacks and was hence laudable. But the older fanatics within the Church had also been able to offer compelling reasons for their beliefs—they were fighting for Truth, immortal souls were at stake, and so forth. Even when they professed to accept these premises, the reformers still rejected the conclusions. Later, however, they accepted the conclusions quite eagerly when these same attitudes and methods were put in the service of different causes. In retrospect this appears to be another form of progressive dishonesty—they simply lacked a commitment to the Church, without admitting so.

One of the continuing scandals of the unreformed Church was the *odium theologicum,* the intemperance with which theologians often denounced works originating outside their own schools. This tendency has merely been exacerbated in the new Church; radical theologians either ignore or treat with great contempt the writings of moderates and conservatives (see, for example, Anselm Atkins' treatment of Henri de Lubac[24]), and religious debate is often carried on amidst a bitterness worthy of the Reformation polemicists. (One common form is to imply that one's opponents are not even worthy of serious consideration. Thus Mary Daly refers to "the styles and games of academic theologians."[25])

The category of heresy was one which reformers hoped to downgrade considerably in the Church, since they believed that it was a convenient tool of the fanatics, a substitute for thought, a smear word, a way of discouraging originality. Yet Michael Novak characterizes American Catholics as Jansenists and Manichees, because of certain of their unprogressive attitudes,[26] and in doing so he is simply expressing a reformer's commonplace—nearly every Catholic liberal can talk at some length about the presence of these ancient heresies in the American Church. Inevitably the suspicion arises that Catholic radicals do not really object to the Holy Office mentality, which is ever vigilant towards heresy and ready to censure, but merely want to alter the content of the categories. They have their own heretics to condemn.

In 1969 Archbishop Robert E. Lucey of San Antonio expressed extreme hawkish sentiments about the Vietnam War in an address to the National Conference of Catholic Charities. A number of delegates to the conference tried unsuccessfully to have his address expunged from the official proceedings.[27] Archbishop Thomas A. Connolly of Seattle made similar remarks at the Jesuits' Seattle University commencement exercises, and the University administration and faculty decreed that at future commencements he was not to speak at all.[28] Apparently, in the reformed Church there will be freedom of speech for everyone but archbishops. In St. Louis two sets of parents who opposed compulsory sex-education were required to remove their children from a parish school.[29] In the same city a high school run by progressive nuns requires a "loyalty oath" from its faculty because some teachers sided with dissident conservative students and parents.[30]

Because it enjoys substantial support, because it has enjoyed generally favorable publicity in the secular media, and because it seeks power, Catholic radicalism now forms a kind of anti-establishment which is also itself an establishment. As such it is inevitably doomed to employ at least some of the dishonest and coercive tactics which all establishments use, although it will probably use them more sparingly than the establishment which it opposes. Catholic radicals evidence their lack of worldly sophistication in their apparent ignorance of a modern sociological commonplace—the Iron Law of Oligarchies, which states that elite groups of individuals will always dominate communities and institutions, even those with apparently democratic structures. Catholic radicals who breathlessly anticipate a coming age of religious anarchism, an ecclesiastical classless society, will in time discover that they have perhaps exchanged a defined, publicly identifiable hierarchy for a covert, elusive hierarchy which refuses even to acknowledge its own authority.

It is probably true that the great majority of human beings, both now and in the past, as well as in the foreseeable future, desire authoritative leaders, at least in certain areas of life, and this seems as true among liberal, educated, forward-looking persons as among the general population. (Among such individuals there is now an almost constant complaint about the absence of "true leadership," both in secular politics and in the Church.) When legally constituted hierarchial authority loses its status, two other kinds of authority emerge to fill the vacuum: charismatic authority—the rule of saints and prophets; and learned authority—the rule of scholars and experts. Both types of authority have already emerged within the American Church.

When progressive Catholics discovered that they could no longer look to their bishops and pastors for needed guidance, they began looking to certain conspicuous individuals for this same guidance, and the outer boundaries of their lives came to be set not by laws or traditions or official pronouncements, but by the personal odysseys of special individuals. Some followed Episcopal Bishop James A. Pike in his wanderings from orthodoxy through rational scepticism to a fashionable (though for him anguished) belief in the occult. Many followed Harvey Cox into sober, bland secularism, then out again into a love of fantasy and ritual. Others went with Daniel Callahan from a moderate, basically orthodox reformism to the discovery that almost everything having to do with religion was meaningless, or with Michael Novak into a deepening flirtation with the New Left and the youth culture, followed by a growing disillusionment with both. Some stood as moderate reformers with Bishop James P. Shannon, then despaired and left the Church when he did. In each case the "radicalization" of the revered leader led the disciples to disillusionment also.

Since the Council, radical Catholics have found culture heroes, although proclaiming their desire to live freely and to liberate themselves from all authority. Sometimes these followers were thoughtful and critical; like most disciples, they were more often enthusiasts and desperate seekers after certainty. In the

47

years of reform many individuals have had their attitudes and values formed primarily by their last book read, their last conference attended, the latest pronouncement of a radical guru. Some gurus have been reluctant to play the role, but others have assiduously cultivated it and have regularly offered their own spiritual and intellectual migrations as a needed substitute for traditional Christian wisdom. A number of theology classes appear to have been taught from the standpoint of the teacher's own spiritual and intellectual crises, and there is probably a great deal of truth in the conservative charge that many young persons have been alienated from the Church by priests' and teachers' projection of their own problems onto their students, their obsessive dwelling on their own frustrations, doubts, and cynicisms. This is indoctrination in every way comparable to orthodox indoctrination.

Catholic radicals are not above protecting their favored ideals from potentially damaging attacks. Thus Father Richard P. McBrien, a Roman Catholic admirer of Bishop John Robinson, disposes of the bishop's critics easily. They are engaged in "philosophical nit-picking" which is "totally irrelevant and misses the whole point of Robinson's theological concerns." [31] Michael Novak writes of Harvey Cox's *The Secular City* that "the appropriate response to it was not argument but changed perspective, not caviling but a conversion of viewpoint." [32] Criticism becomes "nit-picking" and "caviling" and can thus be disposed of in advance and discouraged. A new magisterium is being formed.

In the mid-1950's the Catholic chaplain at Princeton, the Dominican Father Hugh Halton, was disaccredited by the university because of his attacks on various faculty members whom he regarded as atheistic or anti-religious. Catholic conservatives denounced the university's action as a violation of religious freedom and insisted that the priest was being persecuted merely because he told the truth. Catholic liberals, however, upheld the university's actions. The chaplain, they argued, had an obligation to conduct himself in the proper academic manner, respecting divergent viewpoints, arguing civilly and moderately, in fact accepting his status as a guest in the university. However, in 1969 the radical Jesuit Daniel Berrigan was similiarly disaccredited by the Cornell administration because of his involvement with student groups which were considered disruptive. He had also made public slighting remarks about the Cornell administration and faculty.[33] Father Berrigan, however, continued to be a radical Catholic hero, and support for him took almost the precise form which had been declared invalid in the case of Father Halton.

A similar aura of inviolability attached to the late Bishop Pike. When he pronounced the Trinity and the Virgin Birth as "incredible," religious radicals hailed him for his honesty and his clearsightedness. When he claimed to communicate with the dead in seances, however, the approved liberal attitude was silence. Bishop Pike's beliefs were to be respected, and it was considered rude to question them. (Radicals in effect refused to criticize anyone on the Left. Thus James Kavanaugh, whose writings were hysterical, vulgar, and sensational, was treated as a serious thinker.)

Although the radicals have made use of the press to gain for themselves a stature and a following that they otherwise would not have, they resent a critical press when it does not favor them. Father McBrien, a progressive theologian who did not

49

approve the death-of-God theology enjoying a brief vogue in the late 1960's, complained that only the attention given it in the mass media kept that movement alive.[34] However, the same could be said of virtually every other aspect of reform, although this is a fact reformers have generally preferred to ignore. Henry ten Kortenaar, reporting on the Dutch Church to *Commonweal's* readers, sounded like a press agent for the Curia in noting that Cardinal Bernhard Alfrink feared "hasty," "inaccurate," and "sensational" reporting and asked for "caution" and "objectivity."[35]

By identifying hypocrisy and phariseeism solely with those in established positions of authority, radicals have often truncated the wider meaning of the Gospel and reduced it to a partisan weapon. They recognize the pharisee in the alcoholic, racist, graft-taking ward politician who passes the collection plate on Sunday but not in the blue-jeaned college student, sneering at the hypocrisy of his parish, who sells drugs and pressures his girl-friend to have an abortion. They see the money-changer in the pastor who unceasingly demands funds to build a plush rectory but not in the black "leader" who disrupts worship to demand a monetary payment for past suffering and who may or may not intend to use the money to help his people.

The most striking examples of charismatic authority in the Church since the Council have been the religious and laymen who have on several occasions protested the Vietnam War by rifling draft files, destroying their contents, and then accepting prison as a price of their witness. Many liberals who admire the courage of these actions argue that the tactics are misconceived, or that what is significant when done by a few for the sake of dramatization cannot substitute for the more routine work of politics which must be done by the many. Yet some of these same liberals also feel profoundly disquieted, even guilty, at their own failure to follow the lead of the Berrigan brothers. It is of the nature of charismatic authority precisely to make demands on the conscience which the individual does not feel entirely free to reject. Charismatic, or prophetic, authority is potentially the most repressive of all, since it exercises an almost hypnotic attraction over the believer and since its spiritual power invites the destruction of all the disciple's laboriously constructed categories of ethical belief. Daniel Berrigan himself is said to be very impatient with those who fail to follow his example.[36]

For some radical Catholics the essence of Christianity has become intimately linked with the beliefs and actions of a few charismatic leaders, whose example and pronouncements are treated with the respect which the ultra-orthodox reserve for papal encyclicals. Such persons, despite their insistence, do not seek freedom but merely a new kind of authoritarianism. Thus a former priest can write that "Perhaps the future of the Church is one and the same as the future of the Fathers Berrigan, Melville, Groppi, and Wenderoth,"[37] and this is scarcely different from the old tendency to equate the Church with the hierarchy. Yet it is a formulation to which many radicals would apparently subscribe.

No religion can exist without authority at some point, and many radicals who have rejected the force of hierarchy and tradition, indeed of any thing external to the individual, propose the Holy Spirit as the sole authority on whom believers should rely. Rosemary Ruether, whose theology is especially emphatic on this point, says: "We must then be able to see the death of God,

51

that is to say, the incredibility of our religious tradition, as the present work of the Holy Spirit . . . even the Church itself . . . now being made dead and lifeless by the power of the Holy Spirit." [38] Father Eugene Kennedy, a Maryknoll psychologist, says that "Right now in history the impulse of the Spirit is to break open the mold in which successful Catholicism finds itself." [39] There are, of course, no objective standards by which the work of the Holy Spirit can be discerned, and those who appeal to his authority are in effect asking that their own superior sensitivity, even their holiness, be recognized. The Holy Spirit is here put to partisan use, in that those who do not find the religious tradition incredible, or who do not regard the sickness of the Church as a good thing, are told, with hidden but real arrogance, that they simply misunderstand the will of God in this age. A good many Catholic radicals have presumed precisely to read the mind of God in their struggles to mount a counter-authority to that of the hierarchy.

Most reformers have been more modest, however, and the kind of authority now emerging is more commonly the authority of the expert or the scholar, who does not necessarily claim a spiritual superiority over his fellow Catholics but does claim a superior knowledge and a deeper understanding. Here the fundamental contradiction of *aggiornamento* is evident—that reforms which were designed to make men free were imposed either by hierarchical decree or the prestige of experts, who unceasingly told ordinary believers (including some with a good measure of traditional learning) that their ideas about liturgy, theology, the spiritual life, were essentially erroneous and in need of radical change.

Father Gregory Baum, unlike many radicals, has been almost

entirely free of the urge to condemn those who disagree with him, and his theological expositions have always been made in a spirit of moderation, patience, and good will. Yet his essential stance, in explaining the new theology to the general Catholic public, has been authoritarian. "There is no evidence," he writes, "for thinking that religion is imposed on human life by a gifted person. . . . Religion is . . . man's own self-understanding and his relationship to his human and cosmic environment." Those who believe otherwise have a "hangup." [40] Elsewhere he rejoices that, working independently of each other, "American Catholic theologians" (he cites four, including himself) have discovered that "divine transcendence does not refer . . . to God's independent existence in a supernatural world . . . does not refer to a supreme being . . . rather, to the deepest dimension of human history and the cosmos." [41] In these brief sentences he seems to dispose of both the traditional Christian concept of God and the very possibility of divine revelation, as this concept has been understood. These positions are no doubt defensible. What is not defensible is the implication, which is even more clear in the work of theologians less irenic than Father Baum, that these conclusions, having been reached by certified theologians, have a kind of definite and certain character which only the backward or stubborn will resist. Reformers who encourage the laity systematically to question the decrees of the hierarchy or traditional catechisms rarely encourage them to question the speculations of modern theologians.

Often new theology is said to be a rejection of dogma, yet Father Arthur Gibson, another Canadian theologian, insists that ". . . no intelligent attitude can be assumed to any partial phenomenon . . . unless the imminence of this crucial breakthrough to species-consciousness is accorded full importance as inevitable . . . ," [42] and with these words a highly speculative and tentative theory is elevated to a certainty. Sister Louis Gabriel, a theologian writing a critique of the Oberammergau passion play, casually observes that "to love their fellow men more and build a better world, for that is what the Gospel is about," [43] and her prestige as a scholar is put behind a highly simplified understanding of the Scripture, which she does not trouble to argue but apparently expects her readers to accept on her scholarly authority. Progressive theologians are by no means wary of such dogmatizing, and a great deal of the new theology has found its way to wide acceptance simply on the insistently repeated appeal to authority: "Modern theologians believe . . . modern theologians doubt . . . modern theologians have discovered . . ."

Theologians and other intellectuals working on religious problems are understandably hyper-conscious of their new freedom and their new prestige. But they do not often look beyond these conditions, and they have especially not attempted seriously to define their place in the total Church. Father Charles Curran, President of the Catholic Theological Society of America, looks to the day when theology will leave the seminary for the university campuses, and be free of undue hierarchical control. "Theology," he says, "best serves the Church when it is allowed to develop as an academic discipline with its own academic integrity." [44] Those who seek the security and autonomy of an academic theology must recognize the price—that the theologian may well cease to be a special figure, an accepted officer, in the Church and will have a life and an identity outside the religious community. His role will be analogous to that of the political scientist in civil society—generally ignored, given no

54

authority beyond that of the common citizen, occasionally called upon for advice and illumination, possessed of an expertise which the community utilizes only when it chooses and under its own conditions.

Few post-conciliar theologians have asked whether they have any responsibility to the community of believers who are expected to give them spiritual and material support. To say that a theologian best serves the community when he follows his own insights is to vest those insights with a virtual infallibility; it implies that the community of believers has no values, needs, principles, or traditions which must be respected. At a time when progressive religious thought places a heavy emphasis on life in community, it makes the theologian into a *laissez-faire* entrepreneur answerable to no one, and part of no community or tradition. If the test of a bishop's authority must be his willingness to serve the needs of his people, and to listen to them, why should the theologian's authority not be tested in the same way? And if the theologian is permitted to define the community's needs as he sees fit, sometimes contrary to what the majority of the community thinks are its needs, then bishops surely have the same right. (The Dutch theologian Paul Brand indicates the drive for power motivating some intellectuals when he laments that "the walls of the ecclesiastical Jericho have not collapsed in spite of all the theological trumpets." [45])

What is often called the "revolt of the laity" in the Church is in reality closer to a revolt of the experts, who use a democratic rhetoric to mask an elitist conception of religious reform. These experts have a constituency—a minority of educated laity in a few of the more advanced Western nations—who support them enthusiastically, look to them for leadership the bishops cannot provide, and sometimes urge them on to greater daring. The remainder of the Church is in varying degrees indifferent, uninformed, bewildered, sceptical, wary, fearful, or hostile concerning these same experts.

A fair warning of the aristocracy of the future is given by Arthur Deegan, an employee of the archdiocese of Detroit who was commissioned to do a "feasibility study" for a national pastoral council. Finding the need for such a council urgent, Dr. Deegan also remarked that the spirit of renewal is not as widespread "as it ought to be" and calls for a "monumental task of education-orientation." Therefore, the projected council would have to be "representative" but not "democratic." Sometimes it "may even have to go counter to the 'grass-roots' wishes if that popular opinion is unchristian . . ." [46] The call for a council and the warning about democracy are both well taken. But progressives have not even begun to probe the question how, once traditional clerical authority is de-emphasized, power to determine what is "unchristian" can be lodged in a body of individuals who are not answerable to anyone for their decisions. This is merely a formula for a new hierarchy.

The experts and their constituency, who together comprise a religious "new class" comparable to the "new class" of progressive suburbanites which is at present bidding for secular political influence, have formulated an analysis of present conditions in the Church which, if accepted, virtually guarantees its own ascendancy for the foreseeable future. This mythology is based on a core of truth, though much exaggerated: "The masses of believers are almost wholly ignorant of the nature of real Christianity, because they have been deliberately kept as spiritual children by an authoritarian hierarchy. They must cling to the old Church for the sake of emotional security. Through research, bold speculation, and radical life experiences a small but increasing number of individuals has begun to discover the genuine meaning of the Gospel for modern times, although the hierarchy tries to suppress them and the majority of believers will not heed them.

"Christianity itself cannot survive, however, nor individual Christians attain authentic life, unless these new prophets are listened to. The principal means by which the Church will be saved is the charismatic witness of men like Daniel Berrigan, the radical theologizing of individuals like Rosemary Ruether, and the transmission of these same acts and ideas to a larger public through the schools, progressive religious journalism, and radical preachers."

The rise of a "future-oriented" theology, in which God is found only at the end of history, in which man's principal religious task is the creation of a better world, and in which an attachment to tradition and stability is a denial of the core meaning of the Gospel, thus gives the religious radical an unassailable eminence in the Church, quite comparable to the eminence given the pope by the doctrine of papal infallibility. By definition the radical is always more Christian than the conservative, precisely because he is forward-looking. By identifying his own optimistic, mobile, modern temperament with the true spirit of Christianity, the innovator becomes by definition a leader in the Church to whom the masses must look in order to understand the meaning of Christianity for their own day and in order to effect necessary changes in their own lives. If he is sufficiently radical, the prophet can also insulate himself against all possibility of failure or error; for when failures occur, he can explain that the program was simply not radical enough, much in the way that a conservative can always explain prayers not answered on the ground that the petitioner, no matter how earnest, simply lacks sufficient faith.

The majority of believers, if they accept the radicals' analysis of their religious situation, have no choice but to place themselves in bondage to theologians and other experts, and to a few charismatic prophets. The fear which many people have of being "left behind" or of being dupes of the hierarchical establishment has been effectively exploited by many progressive spokesmen, and most of the change which the Council effected—beneficial and otherwise—has simply been imposed by the authority of the new leaders. If believers are wary of ecumenical agreements which seem to abandon traditional beliefs, they are told to dismiss the thought, since the theologians have solved the problem; if they do not find the new liturgy inspirational, they are told that the fault lies with them, because the liturgical experts have constructed good liturgies. Yet consistently these same reformers profess their wish that the people would learn to think for themselves.

Many progressives refuse to admit the elitist character of reform. An exception is Robert Hoyt, editor of the *National Catholic Reporter,* who observes, apropos conservatives' objections to the newer catechisms,

But it is simply true that the religion texts of today are vastly different from those of yesteryear, that progressivist views dominate most Catholic religious and theological training, that in consequence the Catholicism of tomorrow will be something new on earth—and that all this has been accomplished in something less than democratic fashion, by ways and means that eluded standard ecclesiastical safeguards. There *is* a liberal conspiracy, in the sense John Courtney

58

Murray used the word, of a "breathing together"; liberal theologians dominate the public prints, the catechetical training centers, the publishing houses, the professional associations, much of Catholic bureaucracy; they praise each other's books, award each other contracts, jobs, awards and perquisites. There wasn't anything sinister in all this; it wasn't planned, it just happened. . . . But I wouldn't pretend that the situation now obtaining is the consequence of an intellectual victory achieved by the liberals in honest debate, with either bishops or parents as referees. And I doubt that the kids are getting even a sympathtic explanation of what their parents used to believe, much less an option to choose between old-style and new-style Catholicism. Indoctrination is anathema to liberals on principle; but there are ways and ways of indoctrinating. . . .[47]

Radicals are on the whole incredibly insensitive to their own authoritarian attitudes, for the reason all revolutionaries are thus insensitive—they are so obsessed with the oppressiveness of the establishment that any blow struck against it seems automatically a blow for freedom, no matter who strikes it or how it is struck. When Daniel Berrigan says that "I submit it is almost impossible to administer the sacraments according to the intention of Christ without breaking the law of the Church,"[48] he is probably unaware that he is thereby pronouncing invalid the sacraments which countless millions have received devoutly for more than a thousand years; legitimacy is conceded only to the small elite coteries recently sprung up in a few fortunate locations. Given their beliefs, the new leaders are understandably contemptuous of their more lackluster charges, sometimes much more so than any bishop would dare admit being.

James Colaianni, the former lay secretary of the Liturgical Conference, states flatly that "the entire meaning of the liturgy can be summed up with precision in one word—empathy," and "Worship is a word religion should try to forget."[49] The tone of these pronouncements does not invite dialogue and the question is left unasked how Mr. Colaianni, a lawyer by profession, attained such certitude on matters of extreme subtlety and difficulty. The mystique of the expert, however, carries powerful weight. Thus Father Baum can pronounce that "the Christian community . . . is adopting a more dynamic view of man . . . a moral norm is a faithful orientation to personal growth and social reconciliation." Since "the official Church" has not adopted this view, its moral teachings are "inadequate, if not wrong." [50] Quite clearly "the Christian community" is here equated with the small minority of progressive theologians and their followers; both the hierarchy and the masses are in effect read out of this community for heresy.

The crucial battle in this area is being fought over catechetics. Some reactionaries obviously wish to use the catechetics issue as a means of reintroducing the Inquisition into the Church, but this does not obviate the many problems connected with the new catechisms. As Mr. Hoyt has observed, the new books are for the most part drastically different from the old. If they are not actually heretical, as reactionaries charge, they nonetheless effect a sharp break with the Catholic past simply by their silence on many traditional beliefs.

Despite the profound implications of this fact (it will lead to a future Church far different in outlook from the present one), it is impossible to determine how the decision was made to teach this new kind of Catholicism. Clearly it was not made by the bishops, many of whom are highly troubled by the new books. Even more clearly it was not made by popular consensus, since many laymen have also shown themselves quite disturbed over catechetical developments. Instead, insofar as its origins can be discovered, it seems to have originated in a kind of underground consensus of a limited number of largely anonymous individuals in theology schools, publishing houses, and classrooms, who decided among themselves that a new catechetics was needed, and what kind. Few of these persons are accountable to the community of believers, and few have received any kind of mandate from that community.

What is at issue here is not the actual character of the new catechisms, or whether the conservative charges against them are justified, but rather the way in which authority and decision-making operate in the reformed Church. If the essence of the new Catholicism is the freedom of the Christian, his right to make his own conscious decisions without imposition by a hierarchy, then the new catechists clearly have an obligation to give way before parents who object vigorously to what their children (at least pre-adolescent children) are being taught. If the parent believes his child is being harmed spiritually, then only in the rarest cases does the professional have the right to insist on his own authority above that of the parent. At the very least the Catholic schools have an obligation to provide a pluralism of catechetic approaches, so that parents who desire a conservative formation for their children can obtain it. A more deformed kind of authority can scarcely be imagined than that of the "expert" who decides that a parent is incompetent to guide his own children's development and who intervenes to alter this development in accord with his own convictions. Potentially the new catechetics, taught by militantly progressive teachers, can have the effect of seriously alienating children from their parents, whose religious beliefs are easily made to seem foolish, backward, and pernicious.

An instructive example of this covert but very real authoritarianism is the critical evaluation of the newer catechisms by Sheila Moriarty, a "catechetical expert." (Since this is a quite new status in the Church it is not at all clear how individuals become catechetical experts, and to some extent it appears to be a self-defined competence.) Miss Moriarty consistently favors books which equate Christianity with ethics, and is generally critical of those which emphasize a supernatural dimension of existence. She is especially taken with a high-school text which opens with an analysis of *West Side Story* and then moves on to an encounter with "the man Jesus." The resurrection of Jesus is described as ". . . when man, who tends to be closed to God, achieves complete openness to God in the total response of the man Jesus." Christ is seen as "a pragmatist, a man of action, a doer." She also approves another book which "appears to have no specifically 'religious' content," and is constantly opposed to all explicit attempts to relate the here-and-now world to a transcendent dimension. Her examination of the range of catechetical works reveals that "only a few reflect a reverent and authentic understanding of the Christian life." [51]

How Miss Moriarty has achieved a more authentic understanding of the Christian life than those other "catechetical experts" who authored the books she dislikes is not made clear. Yet presumably the character of Catholic belief for the coming generation has to a large extent been already determined by individuals like Miss Moriarty, passing judgment as she passes judgment, in places to which neither the bishop nor the concerned parent has access. What Miss Moriarty pronounces dogmatically as either bad or good catechetics is in reality the

adoption of certain highly controversial conclusions of certain modern theologians, which in no sense have been formally accepted by the community of believers.

Yet in countless ways the bewildered Catholic is now told that he must accept the opinions of the experts. Whereas the old hierarchy could dispose of dissenters by pronouncing them "heretical," "disloyal," "undocile," or "lacking in faith," the new authorities can dismiss them as "ignorant," "backward," "fearful of change," "insecure," or indeed as "lacking in faith." A test of the openness of any leader is his willingness to listen sincerely to his people, and this is a test which very few progressive scholars can pass. Eugene Schallert, a Jesuit sociologist, knows that those who believe in the Real Presence are "bureaucratic Catholics" who care only about formulas, not deeper reality.[52] William DuBay, a former priest, wants to abolish all religion classes for children and allow only parents to teach their offspring. But this very democratic suggestion is then vitiated by a quite detailed exposition of exactly what and how the parents should teach, even to the ideal size of their catechetical groups.[53] John G. Milhaven, a Jesuit ethician, looks to a day when ethics will be largely a dead discipline. The behavioral sciences will give answers to ethical questions—how to achieve a healthy sexuality, and so on. "For the new ethics, the only pertinent specialist in the matter at hand is the man of science and professional experience."[54] Catholics have apparently freed themselves from the bondage of religious authority only in order to deliver themselves to the bondage of scientists and pseudo-scientists. (It is characteristic of Catholic radicals' lack of worldly awareness that such predictions are made at precisely the moment when many secular radicals are deeply troubled over the manipulative power of the sciences and the social sciences in many areas of human life.)

Under the rubric of freedom and democracy, radicalism in the Church, at least on the part of some, can be seen as a drive by the modern aristocracy—the educated, indispensable class of experts—to wrest power away from a traditional, pre-modern, mystic ruling group. The same transfer of power has to a great extent already occured in secular life. Whatever its considerable benefits, it has little to do with democracy. Admirers of the new expert class do not object at all to authority, only to certain kinds of authority. Thus those who, against Paul VI's birth-control declaration, asserted indignantly that "The pope should stay out of the bedroom. This is a matter for the marriage partners to decide," are quite often willing to entertain thoughts of compulsory family limits, imposed by the state on the advice of population experts. Liberal Catholics who deplore the influence—both hidden and open—which the Church is able to exert in some communities are usually quite sanguine over the similar power of the giant private foundations, which by giving or withholding money can greatly affect the course of education or social reform. Elise Boulding, a sociologist and Protestant lay woman, tells other lay women that the nuclear family dwelling in a private home is no longer feasible and has many pernicious effects. Community life is the necessary wave of the future, and she apparently gives conservatives little opportunity to choose in the matter.[55] So long as values and policies are determined by educated, progressive, "open-minded" experts, many liberal Christians are quite willing to accept authoritative guidance.

If the existence of this new power group is acknowledged, which it rarely is, it is often defended on the ground that it is genuinely more democratic, more humane and responsive, less repressive than older forms of authority. This is probably true, although its greater sophistication gives this group far more potential for long-term dominance. However, even under present very tentative conditions, the new leadership sometimes shows its authoritarian character, its concern to preserve its own power against effective challenge. William DuBay sees only one possible plan for renewal. (1) Abolish church-going (he makes no provision for those who would like to continue attending), and (2) then burn down the churches. Those who resist such drastic measures are "playing the devil's game." [56] (The devil, although generally abolished by the radicals, has his uses on occasion.) Anselm Atkins wishes to declare illegitimate any future council which does not include Protestants and Eastern Orthodox,[57] thus effectively denying Catholics the right to meet with each other on common problems. Frederick Franck, portraying the ideal pope of the future, finds that "he discouraged all desperate attempts to impose traditional doctrine by sheer repetition or by detailed dogmatic elaboration," [58] which apparently means that in this purified Church conservative theologians will be harassed and forbidden to do their work. Brother Gabriel Moran, perhaps America's most notable catechetics expert, suggests limiting religious instruction to adults,[59] although a majority of Catholic parents probably want their children to be instructed. Jesuit Father Joseph Fichter proposes that marriage for bishops be mandatory.[60] In commenting on those who support Paul VI's birth-control encyclical, *Humanae Vitae,* Daniel Callahan observed that "there is much sense in the traditional corollary that they should have an informed conscience; a lot of mischief is done in the name of conscience." [61]

Father Gerard Sloyan proposes that in choosing permanent deacons the Church should exclude "retreat buffs, Serra Club members, rectory hangers-on, retired soldiers, corporation executives, law-enforcement officers, dedicated anti-Communists." [62] It apparently does not occur to Father Sloyan that some of these people, who have given considerable service to the Church, might legitimately resent this policy of exclusion; radicals have by now decided that "the open Church" need not include conservatives and that progressive leaders need not fear becoming authoritarian, if it is for a good cause. To this may be added the admiration some Catholics have for the Black Panthers, Students for a Democratic Society, and other groups which seem to advocate violent change. It is not inconceivable that some of these Christians would support a holy war under the proper conditions.

Some of the new leaders also show the familiar tendency to protect themselves from criticism by taking refuge in their offices. When the Dutch Pastoral Council proposed that married priests be subject to the judgment of their parishioners as to their attitudes and competence, Frederick Franck commented: "shades of the Inquisition," [63] although clerical accountability is supposed to be desirable in the new democratized Church. When the National Association of Laymen tried to fire Don Nicodemus, he at first refused to resign, and asserted that legally he could not be ousted,[64] although radicals regard legalism and entrenched, unresponsive leadership as an abomination in the Church. (Nicodemus later resigned.) Monsignor Charles O. Rice, a radical

66

Pittsburgh pastor, suggested that the clergy shortage is caused by the progressive religious' unwillingness to devote themselves to an unworthy laity, "such an awful crew," who are "not worth bothering about," [65] although the Council has presumably set for religious an ideal of service to their people and has supposedly abolished the religious mystique by which some in the Church hold themselves above others. Scarcely veiled in Monsignor Rice's comments is an implied threat—either the laity fall into line with progressive thinking or the clergy will withdraw their services. This is an interesting modern variation on the Interdict. (Following the 1969 Liturgical Week, at which the president, Father Joseph Connelly, referred to non-swingers as "stiff-assed honkies," five members resigned from the board of the Liturgical Conference and the 1970 meeting had to be cancelled because of a drastic decline in enrollment.[66] The leadership apparently did not conclude therefrom that they were unresponsive to the people.)

Probably no belief of the traditional Church is now so scorned as the idea of infallibility, whether of the pope or of the whole Church. Yet without employing the name, radicals often claim for themselves a kind of negative infallibility. They are quite prepared to state dogmatically, and in a way which precludes discussion, what doctrines of the Church are untrue, incredible, pernicious, or inhumane. They generally expect wide assent to these pronouncements, and they regard those who do not assent as fools and the Church's failure to respond as clear evidence of its corruption. An extreme example is William DuBay, who became a liberal hero in 1964 for defying Cardinal James McIntyre by preaching about racial justice. Father DuBay later published a book in which he asserted, virtually without argument, that the Hebrews had abolished religion, that "knowledge of God is not only incredible but inhuman," that "He [God] has no use for churches, . . . exercises of religion are an insult to him . . . ," that "what Christ was after, really, was a group of people that would be an anti-Church. . . ." [67] (The DuBay case is instructive also for a certain kind of reformers' dishonesty which it reveals. Prior to the publication of Father DuBay's book few Catholics realized that the author held such extreme opinions. Support for him in his struggle with Cardinal McIntyre was solicited solely on the ground that he was a sincere priest simply trying to implement the Church's teachings on racial justice.)

Ironically, the power and authority which the new leaders seek is largely invalidated by conditions in the Church which they themselves have essentially created—the new freedom and openness, and the global uncertainty about all matters Catholic. In the past the hierarchy could claim authority on the basis of traditional doctrines which were coherent and universally accepted in the Church. Theologians could compel acceptance of their theories by demonstrating their relevance to traditional beliefs or official pronouncements. Now, when both tradition and established authority are greatly discredited, the authority which any new Catholic leader can claim is of necessity personal authority. In a variety of ways, the new leaders simply assert that they are more learned, more honest, more sensitive, more courageous, more modern, and more "human" than those they criticize. A more arrogant claim can scarcely be imagined.

The dubiousness of these claims to authority derives not only from the present uncertainty and disarray in the Church, but also from the very nature of religion, whose ultimate core of meaning lies beyond all possibility of proof or empirical verification, lies of course in the realm of faith. A theologian, insofar as he attempts to talk about God or about man's ideas of God, necessarily engages in a rather arbitrary procedure. He makes certain crucial choices, based on his own values, which determine the results of his theology. Conservative theologians at least claim an objective "revelation" outside themselves, embodying a message which can be the basis for validating theological speculations. Those who reject this traditional idea of revelation have nothing to substitute except their own insights.

It is thus highly misleading to speak of the "discoveries" of modern theologians, or to imply that after many centuries theologians have at last found the true meaning of religious belief. Theologians do not engage in "research" in the same way that physicists or historians engage in research. Their conclusions are necessarily speculative and necessarily value judgments, and there is no inherent reason for assuming that modern theologians' values are necessarily superior to those of their predecessors. Yet much of the new theology has been presented with an implied theory of private revelation, as though the radical theologian somehow has access to new information about God which traditionalists lack.

Few radical theologians have shown themselves aware of the rather arbitrary character of their own speculations, but the unsatisfactory results of this arbitrariness are often evident. Thus while Gregory Baum gently chastizes traditionalists for their ideas of God and of revelation and their ethical principles, Mary Daly more vigorously chastizes Father Baum for insisting that the divine word was revealed definitively in Jesus. "How does he know this?" she asks.[68] To a thorough secularist, however, Professor Daly's continued interest in theology and God might also seem quite arbitrary and unjustifiable, a chimera. Rosemary Ruether effectively denies all authority to the formal teachings of the Church, but she has an apparently intense faith in the Holy Spirit, a faith which to a non-believer scarcely seems more intelligible or less arbitrary. Many radical theologians seem to want to define the limits of valid belief at precisely the point they themselves happen to inhabit at a given moment. They deny other people the right to believe, while reserving it to themselves.

In one important area the theologian does engage in verifiable research, and that is Scripture studies, which have had an immense impact on almost all aspects of contemporary Church life. Here the scholar may discover that certain beliefs of the Church are in contradiction to the Gospel or are based on misunderstandings of the Gospel, and such conclusions must have crucial relevance to the Church's future course. But a fundamental and very serious problem presents itself. Scripture studies are highly specialized, technical, and arcane. Even the intelligent and educated non-specialist can scarcely evaluate the scholars' work. Of necessity, therefore, Scripture scholars have become an invincible class of intellectual leaders, quite as unassailable in their own territory as nuclear physicists. If a correct understanding of Scripture, elucidated by modern scholarship, is a necessity for modern faith, then believers will be in perpetual bondage to Scripture scholars, required to follow blindly whatever the latest and best research seems to dictate. Clearly religion cannot be so wedded to technical expertise; the illiterate peasant must somehow have access to authentic belief. The whole problem of the scholar's relation to the believing community has scarcely begun to be worked out, but it is a problem which does not seem to interest radicals very much.

Many progressives have shown themselves quite ready to use authority of various kinds, so long as it suits their purposes. Much innovation in the Church has been legitimized in the following manner: (1) appeals to the decrees of Vatican II. When certain of these decrees are discovered to be rather conservative, this shifts to (2) appeals to the "spirit" of Vatican II, which did not get embodied in all the decrees, or to (3) the "spirit of Pope John," whose intentions were so radical that the Council did not begin to probe them. When faced with the traditionalism of this Pope on many questions (see *The Journal of a Soul*), refuge can be sought in (4) Scripture, whose authority exceeds that of all popes and councils. When inconvenient passages about hell or physical resurrection are brought forward, these are explained as peculiarities of the Semitic mind and the burden is shifted to (5) the needs and beliefs of modern man. By this process the traditionalist is bound by the radical to a continual adherence to the authorities, while the radical leaves himself free to go wherever he chooses.

In 1968 Martin Marty had warned Catholics that "whenever it issues in fanaticism, obsession, or crusading spirit, renewal appears not as renewal of Church but as representation of personal problem." [69] Few of the radical reformers listened to this warning, despite the fact that the realities he was referring to were already helping to poison the reform movement. That Professor

71

Marty's warning was quite accurate is suggested by the fact that so many ardent progressives are willing to continue in paths which virtually guarantee the failure of significant reform and the continued disintegration of the Church.

Notes

1. *Commonweal,* Oct. 26, 1962, p. 10.
2. *Ibid.,* Oct. 9, 1964, p. 74.
3. *Ibid.,* June 18, 1965, p. 403.
4. *Ibid.,* Jan. 16, 1970, p. 425.
5. *America,* April 9, 1966, p. 483.
6. *Continuum,* Winter, 1968, p. 729.
7. *National Catholic Reporter,* Nov. 19, 1969, p. 2.
8. Callahan, *Honesty,* p. 108.
9. *Commonweal,* Nov. 14, 1969, p. 226.
10. *Ibid.,* Nov. 8, 1968, p. 224.
11. *Ibid.,* March 28, 1969, p. 34.
12. *America,* April 9, 1966, p. 483.
13. *Ibid.,* p. 484.
14. *The Catholic World,* Sept., 1969, p. 254.
15. *Commonweal,* Feb. 24, 1961, p. 546.
16. *Ibid.,* May 11, 1962, p. 166.
17. *Ibid.,* July 6, 1962, p. 373.
18. *Ibid.,* Jan. 29, 1965, p. 590.
19. Thorman, *The Emerging Layman* (Garden City, 1962), pp. 227-8.
20. *Commonweal,* Oct. 10, 1969, p. 54.
21. *U.S. Catholic,* March, 1968, p. 33.
22. *Look,* Feb. 20, 1968, p. 102.
23. Carling, *Move Over!* (New York, 1969), p. 86.
24. *Commonweal,* May 3, 1968, pp. 211-3.
25. *Ibid.,* Sept. 6, 1968, p. 601.
26. *Generation of the Third Eye,* p. 170.
27. *St. Louis Review,* Oct. 10, 1969, p. 2.
28. *Continuum,* Summer, 1969, pp. 377-9.
29. *St. Louis Post-Dispatch,* Oct. 12, 1969, p. I-1.
30. *Ibid.,* April 9, 1969, p. 1A, 5A: May 14, 1969, p. 23D.

31. *Commonweal,* Sept. 23, 1966, p. 608.

32. *Journal of Ecumenical Studies,* Spring, 1969, p. 229.

33. *St. Louis Review,* Oct. 24, 1969, p. 8; *Jubilee,* Feb., 1968, pp. 28-36.

34. McBrien, *Do We Need the Church?* (New York, 1969), p. 47.

35. *Commonweal,* Feb. 7, 1969, pp. 581-2.

36. Reported by Francine du Plessix Gray, *The New Yorker,* March 14, 1970, pp. 114-5.

37. *Commonweal,* April 3, 1970, p. 79.

38. Ruether, *The Church Against Itself* (New York, 1967), p. 222.

39. *America,* Aug. 22, 1970, p. 85.

40. *Commonweal,* May 15, 1970, p. 212.

41. *St. Louis Review,* June 26, 1970, p. 9.

42. *Commonweal,* Oct. 31, 1969, p. 120.

43. *The Catholic World,* April, 1970, p. 17.

44. *National Catholic Reporter,* July 3, 1970, p. 3.

45. *Ibid.,* Sept. 25, 1970, p. 1.

46. *Ibid.,* Sept. 4, 1970, pp. 3, 4; *St. Louis Review,* Sept. 4, 1970, p. 1.

47. *National Catholic Reporter,* July 10, 1970, p. 15.

48. *U.S. Catholic and Jubilee,* June, 1969, p. 9.

49. Colaianni, *The Catholic Left* (Philadelphia, 1968), pp. 26-7.

50. *St. Louis Review,* July 3, 1970, p. 8.

51. *Worship,* May, 1967, p. 273; Aug.-Sept., 1967, pp. 400-2; Aug.-Sept., 1968, p. 414.

52. Colaianni, *Catholic Left,* p. 99.

53. DuBay, *The Human Church* (Garden City, 1966), pp. 98-105.

54. *Commonweal,* Oct. 31, 1969, pp. 139-40.

55. *St. Louis Post-Dispatch,* April 1, 1970, p. 4F.

56. DuBay, *The Human Church,* p. 49.

57. *Commonweal,* Oct. 31, 1969, p. 154.

58. *Ibid.,* p. 165.

59. *U.S. Catholic and Jubilee,* Jan., 1970, pp. 12-3.

60. *Commonweal,* May 24, 1968, pp. 289-91.

61. *Ibid.,* Aug. 23, 1968, p. 559.

62. Quoted in *Worship,* Dec., 1969, p. 630.

63. *Commonweal,* Feb. 6, 1970, p 503.

64. *St. Louis Review,* Jan. 30, 1970, p. 12.

65. *The Catholic World,* July, 1970, p. 158.

66. See the reports by C. J. McNaspy, S.J., *America,* Oct. 18, 1969, p.

321; and John Deedy, *Commonweal,* Sept. 19, 1969, p. 554, and Feb. 20, 1970, p. 546.

67. DuBay, *The Human Church,* pp. 13, 15, 36, 98, 49.
68. *National Catholic Reporter,* July 10, 1970, p. 12.
69. *America,* Aug. 31, 1968, p. 124.

3.

The Empty Cloister

LIKE so many post-conciliar crises, the clerical-religious crisis should have been predictable, yet no one foresaw it. All the preconciliar criticisms of the religious life converged towards this point: young persons pressured into seminaries and convents before they were old enough to make mature decisions; systematic insulation from worldly influences; rigid life style involving a good deal of self-repression; intense but narrow intellectual formation; an artificial and arduous public image; and so on. An explosion was inevitable, and it was bound to involve a good deal of bizarre behavior as well as new and creative freedom.

Progressives misunderstood the crisis of the religious life about as thoroughly as they misunderstood every other crisis in the conciliar years. First there were assurances that certain reforms which seemed radical (secular dress, life away from the cloister, study at secular universities) could lead only to improvement of the religious vocation and could in no real way conflict with it. Discontented religious who demanded these reforms were regarded as the best kind of religious, truly interested in saving the life and improving it. (An "internationally known theologian" is said to have remarked, after seeing a certain order's new habits, "Build buildings quickly, because young women will storm your novitiate." [1] If his identity can be discovered he is entitled to at least a runner-up award for the most absurd remark of the whole *aggiornamento.*) Above all, would-be reformers insisted that they had no fundamental quarrel with the religious life as such, only with certain aspects of it. Daniel Callahan in 1963 thought it dubious that there was any "attempted secularization of the priest." [2]

It is possible to trace a particular odyssey through which many religious passed in the 1960's and which was archetypal of the interior odyssey experienced by many others: (1) The Discovery of Learning. In the earlier part of the decade many younger religious sought permission for advanced study, preferably on a secular campus. Their superiors were often dubious, but the individual argued that no ultimate conflict was possible between the truths of religion and the truths of reason and that a mature religious would encounter no "temptation" away from the cloister. Education would in fact insure a more effective apostolate. (2) The Discovery of the Poor. A few years after the degree had been won, education and scholarship began to seem effete and unreal, even damaging to the individual's ministry. (These points had been made originally by the superiors a few years previously.) The religious now demanded to take up work in the inner-city, with the poor, again insisting that no conflict between this secular work and the ideals of the order could possibly obtain. Sometimes the order was told by the individual to abandon all its educational activities in order to devote itself entirely to the poor. (3) Secularization. Within a short time the individual in the ghetto began to find the demands of the religious life impossible and fundamentally in conflict with the work undertaken. A thorough embrace of the world was called for, with no particular religious identity either possible or desirable. (4) Ultimate Happiness. Within a few years the former religious married another

76

like-minded soul and founded a family, took a salaried job (or became a housewife), and assumed an existence not very different from that of high-school classmates left behind on entering the cloister twenty years before. Contacts with the poor now became about as peripheral as those of any moderately liberal suburbanite.

Many discontented religious in the 1960's were dishonest with themselves in the same way many progressive laymen were dishonest—they systematically avoided, for a long time, the question whether it was not the whole idea of the religious life, and not simply its abuses, which troubled them. They often reacted quite defensively when this was suggested, and many offered reasons for their departure from the cloister which studiously failed to touch the fundamental issues. Part of the motive was probably to avoid acknowledging the extent of personal crisis. Part of it was also political—a dissident who admitted fundamental scepticism about the enterprise might forfeit the right to prescribe new directions for it.

Instead strenuous attempts were made in some quarters to make the religious life "relevant" to people whom no amount of reform could satisfy. Indeed, the faster the orders reformed, the more members they lost and the fewer recruits they attracted. (In 1969 there was a report from Europe that the more conservative monastic orders were attracting and keeping novices better than the reformed orders. The most advanced and "relevant" groups were gaining almost no one.[3]) For a while, radicals could explain this embarrassing fact by insisting that reform simply was not coming fast enough or that it was more apparent than real. Only at the end of the decade did some of them at last admit that they had little use for the religious life itself, or for the priesthood, and considered reform illusory. (Ton Veerkamp, a Dutch Jesuit whose wish to continue in the priesthood though married was a major *cause célèbre* in Holland a few years ago, now confesses his fear that "there is no point in the Church, whether renewed or not" and "to me the Church is just as irrelevant as Judaism was for Jesus."[4]) In the meantime, however, a great deal of unnecessary bitterness and mistrust had been introduced into the Church—quarrels over reforms which the reformer himself often came to regard as meaningless within a short time. A great deal of misdirected and wasted energy was spent pursuing the chimera of a magically transformed religious life which would hold all dissenters.

Through most of the 1960's dissident religious insisted that their problems were rigid and unsympathetic superiors, archaic rules, narrow apostolates, and so forth. Often they claimed that they wished only to exercise the ministry in a more perfect fashion. Yet the looser the structures became, the more dissatisfied the radicals became. Some of those looking at the situation from the outside saw it more clearly than the religious themselves. Charles Davis commented acerbically, after perusing a *Commonweal* symposium on the "new priest" in 1968, that the crisis of the priesthood was primarily the fact that many of those involved in it had ceased to believe in it, and he severely criticized their general habit of ignoring that fact.[5] The secular radical Paul Goodman, who for a while enjoyed guru status among the young, had suggested the year before that when campus chaplains insisted that students had no interest in theology, they were projecting their own doubts and misreading the mood of the students.[6] It was some time before very many discontented religious would come to acknowledge these insights.

At first, the sudden and intense interest of priests and religious in the social apostolate seemed a great blessing, an extraordinary manifestation of the Spirit, and a tangible grace deriving from the Council. In many ways it still appears so. However, it is now possible to understand the psychology of this social awakening in a way that was not possible in the beginning. George Eliot described the phenomenon over a century ago in *Scenes of Clerical Life:* "No wonder the sick-room and the lazarette have so often been a refuge from the tossings of intellectual doubt—a place of repose for the worn and wounded spirit. Here is a duty about which all creeds and all philosophies are at one; here, at least, the conscience will not be dogged by doubt, the benign impulses will not be checked by adverse theory; here you may begin to act without settling one preliminary question." [7]

When religious (and laymen) were first becoming acutely involved with social action in the earlier 1960's, religious justifications were usually given as the explicit motive for their involvement. For many, however, this involvement simply began the abandonment of all or most of their religious beliefs. Often this was explained as the discovery of "the autonomy of the secular" —that it is not necessary to have religious motives for loving one's neighbor; the neighbor's need is alone sufficient. No doubt for many persons this was true. However, a contrary psychology seems to have been at least as prevalent—many religious became socially aware because they sensed their religious commitments slipping. Social involvement was on their part an attempt to salvage a meaning for their vocations. The accuracy of this surmise is indicated in the fact that not a few ex-religious, after passing successfully through their crisis of secularization, exchanged intense social involvement for a conventional job and marriage.

At first, all defectors from the religious life were treated by progressives as great idealists, as they usually presented themselves. In the post-conciliar years it became common for priests, upon deciding to leave the ministry, to summon press conferences, issue statements condemning the Church's inhuman character, sometimes to write books or go on the lecture circuit. Some ex-priests achieved national and international reputations in this way. Usually their critique of the Church was essentially valid—inadequate concern for the poor and for social problems generally, overly rigid and immobile structure, inhuman procedures, and so on. Often, however, these jeremiads were accompanied by the announcement of the priest's forthcoming marriage or that the marriage had already taken place. Liberals professed not to be embarrassed by these coincidences; some of the more credulous stated boldly that the rejection of the priesthood for idealistic reasons was wholly distinct from the desire to marry. Others developed a more sophisticated argument—the priest had wanted to leave the Church for some time but only found the strength when at last he encountered a sympathetic woman. (One former priest admitted in print that the girl he married had set out to win him before she even knew him, except as celebrant of the sacred mysteries. She set up phony interviews with him solely for this purpose, and finally succeeded.[8] He found this strategy endearing.)

Struggling against the negative conservative myth of the ex-priest, the progressives have constructed a counter-myth of their own, which also has power and a certain measure of truth. In this counter-view departing religious are quasi-saints. They are the people who took most seriously the high ideals of Christianity and were thus most disillusioned with the reality they experienced

80

in the Church. (At liberal-Catholic cocktail parties in the later 1960's it was inevitable for someone to state that "You know, it's the best seminarians who leave." Usually the source of this information was a seminarian who had left.) Indeed, just as the conservative myth requires a typology of good guys and bad guys—faithful priests who stay versus renegades who abandon ship—so that radical typology sees little of good in those who remain behind. The psychologist Carlo Weber, a former Jesuit, implies that those who do not leave are motivated by nostalgia, insecurity, false hopes for the future, or a misguided desire not to abandon their friends.[9] Norbert Rigali, a social scientist from whom one might expect a sophisticated analysis, instead writes of a "theology of the walkout" in which everyone who leaves is human, sensitive, and courageous, while those who stay are fear-ridden and concerned with structures rather than people.[10] His account seems modelled on pre-conciliar vocation pamphlets, with the roles of the "generous" and the "selfish" simply reversed. Father Eugene Schallert, whose objectivity seems open to question in the light of his dogmatic negativism about the traditional Church, presents research which purports to show departing priests as free, courageous, and religious, chiefly motivated by the failure of the Church to reform itself. But the experience of many Catholics suggests that priests who leave often do so precisely because of change, which has destroyed their secure status and made it impossible for them to respect the Church any longer. Father Schallert's findings are predictably given sympathetic attention in the secular press, while the more unflattering analyses of ex-priests by the Jesuit psychiatrist James Gill are largely ignored.[11]

Among radicals there has been a virtual conspiracy against

81

frank, deglamorized, objective discussion of the clerical crisis. Father Gregory Baum offers as "a profound remark" a statement by one of his colleagues that young people would be scandalized if those remaining in the Church were critical of those who left.[12] Yet many of those who left have made second careers for themselves hurling biting, contemptuous criticisms at the Church and its members. (An ex-Paulist, for example, presents his former brethren as egocentric, adolescent, materialistic, cold-hearted, and trivial-minded.[13]) In the radicals' philosophy no one in the Church, from the pope down, is to be immune from severe criticism, if this seems warranted. Ex-religious, however, have often been treated by their sympathizers as sacrosanct persons whom it is churlish and uncharitable to criticize. Defecting priests and religious in fact enjoy a privileged position in this regard—they can write books, appear on television, issue statements to the press, or relate stories about their past lives which paint their former superiors and colleagues in black colors. The superiors, however, are barred from contradicting these assertions and may not publicly release any information which would detract from the ex-religious' reputation. A rather one-sided account of these departures has thus accumulated, and, despite the human penchant for self-justification, Catholic progressives have been inclined to accept every ex-religious' story at face value.

In the radical ideology priests and religious are encouraged, through a kind of fanatic individualism, to believe that "personal happiness" and "personal fulfillment" alone are relevant considerations in deciding whether to leave and marry. There is little emphasis on any obligation the individual might owe the community to which he ministers. No one knows how many promising renewal programs—in parishes and dioceses, in universities, in religious orders—have been blighted by the sudden departure, at a crucial point, of the individual leading the program. Often these departures reveal that the leader, while appearing enthusiastic and committed, has been planning a departure for some time. (In 1969 there was a dispute at a Catholic college between the local bishop and a group of priests, students, and adult laymen who had been conducting an experimental liturgy. The local pastor, whose church was used, tried to ban the liturgy. After many protests the bishop withdrew his objections, and the pastor was removed. There was a great deal of talk about the beautiful sense of community experienced by the controversial group and their determination not to be split up. Almost immediately after their victory, however, two of the priest-leaders announced their departures from the ministry and their forthcoming marriages. Both left town. One of those leaving had been the principal spokesman for the group in its struggle with the authorities. Both had apparently been planning their departures the whole time the dispute raged.)

Part of the malaise, the listlessness and cynicism, which now affect the Church can be traced to the uncertainty and often unacknowledged mistrust which exists between progressive priests and laymen, who may also like and admire each other. Often a layman discovers that a priest with whom he can communicate and on whom he depends to a degree for spiritual leadership simply disappears one day, leaving a gaping void. There is an unavoidable mistrust which grows up as the layman listens to a sermon or assists at Mass—does this priest really believe what he is saying and doing; is he merely planning a way to depart without excessive trauma; does he have any real interest in this congregation? Too often a notable progressivism has simply been a

THE DECLINE AND FALL OF RADICAL CATHOLICISM

prelude to abandoning the community, often without a farewell word or much thought for projects left unfinished. (The archetypal instance of this situation was the marriage in 1969 of Auxiliary Bishop James P. Shannon of St. Paul-Minneapolis. His resignation from the priesthood deprived American progressives of their leading spokesman in the hierarchy. It tended to discredit the causes which he championed, since it was possible once again for conservatives to conclude smugly that the desire to marry is the real motive behind clerical liberalism. And whatever his intentions, or whatever the real circumstances of his marriage, he acted irresponsibly towards the many progressives throughout the country who considered him a leader. They were left accusing the hierarchy of persecuting him for his liberal views, while he himself was planning his laicization and marriage. His defenders were given no hint of his plans, and suddenly discovered that they were fighting against the "firing" of someone who was actually resigning.)

Thus it is not sufficient to blame the entire crisis on the hierarchy alone, for refusing to permit a married priesthood. Given this situation in the Church, the priest also has an obligation to the community and cannot make his personal happiness the sole criterion of his decision. On the whole, a priest's laicization is perhaps like a layman's divorce—necessary sometimes, but always a tragedy for those involved.

When personal fulfillment is given as the major justification for clerical marriage, it then becomes relevant to inquire whether priests who marry achieve this fulfillment. Many ex-religious who are enthusiastic over the married life were a few years ago equally enthusiastic over the religious life. They perhaps originally entered the novitiate or seminary with the joy and optimism with which they now enter marriage. Some of them have a highly romanticized and unhealthy concept of marriage as a relationship of mystical fulfillment where no element of selfishness, frustration, narrowness, or dulling routine enters in, where no demands are placed on the individual which could possibly repress his freedom and self-fulfillment as he conceives it. (The objections which some former religious have to cloistered life suggest that the discipline of marriage will also be irksome to them.) The religious life has always attracted some individuals who are seeking an ideal existence free from vexing human limitations. When they discover that this life is not to be found in the cloister, it merely compounds the problem to encourage them to look for the same thing in marriage.

Among religious who have spoken openly about their personal odysseys there is a good deal of evidence that discontent has deeper roots than the acknowledged desire to marry. Conservatives, who are always shocked and offended by religious defections, accept as dogma the idea that someone who leaves cannot have been a good religious to begin with. Now many ex-religious acknowledge this charge in effect. In the cloister they found prayer boring and sterile and simply abandoned it. They rejected celibacy, in spirit if not in practice. They freely violated rules as it suited them. Often they experienced profound doubts about the most fundamental beliefs of the Church. (This is now admitted by William DuBay.[14]) They had in fact ceased to be religious before deciding to marry. Radicals, who exclude from consideration any argument based on faith (in the traditional sense), suggest that this inner apostasy indicates the collapse of the religious life as a valid ideal. But conservatives may be correct in citing the unanimous opinion of the great spiritual teachers that discipline, a regimen, a strategy for surviving the dry seasons, are indispensable to the religious life. Many religious believed otherwise; they seem to have largely proven themselves wrong.

Much of this concern for personal fulfillment is valid and healthy, precipitating the elimination of meaningless and burdensome debris from the past. But in retrospect the demand for personal fulfillment can be seen as also a negative sign from many people, an indication that without their being aware of it fully the whole religious life had become meaningless. The religious life as classically structured was the antithesis of personal fulfillment. The religious was supposed to shed all vestiges of individual personality in order to blend with the community. Personal desires were irrelevant. Ideally the religious could accept privation and injustice, even from his superiors, because of the intensity of his spiritual life and the fulfillment he found in apostolic work.

It was this view of the religious life against which so many individuals reacted strongly in the post-conciliar years, and it was in many ways a needlessly harsh and inhumane ideal. Yet Catholic radicals who denounce such ideals, and religious who refuse to live by them, often see beauty in these concepts when they encounter them in other contexts, especially in politically revolutionary groups. There is in fact nothing wrong in principle with this concept of the religious life, so long as it is linked to a meaningful higher purpose, either the service of others or the search for God. No great good was ever achieved without total self-sacrificing dedication on the part of some people, who gave no thought to personal fulfillment except as they found it in this service. The desire of so many religious to fulfill themselves and to express their individuality is on the whole a sign that the cause they serve has ceased to hold them, and thus they find the sacrifices demanded of them oppressive. The crisis of the religious life was from the beginning a crisis of faith primarily, and discontent over lesser issues ultimately stemmed from this.

The demand for clerical marriage at this particular time confirms therefore the Church's classic belief that those who are truly devoted to the priesthood will accept gladly the sacrifices placed upon them. While this does not argue that the Church should necessarily impose these sacrifices, it does suggest a certain hesitation about allowing marriage as the solution to the present clerical crisis. Even priests who are not radical find their faith shakier than it was five years ago. They are much less certain in their ministries, much less convinced of the need for what they do, confused as to their proper roles. In so unsatisfying a situation, the solace of marriage naturally has a much stronger attraction than it once did.

The mythology of the dissident priest pictures him typically as a man thirsting to serve his fellow man, especially the poor, but thwarted in his ambitions by an uncomprehending institution, which finally forces him to resign in order to pursue the will of God in the world. Like all myths, this one inevitably describes some realities, but it also obscures a great deal more. Ex-priests seem to have most conspicuously found employment in education and social work, both of which tend to confirm the stereotype of the man concerned to serve his fellow human beings. Yet usually the priest who begins work as a lay teacher or a social worker was in similar work while still a priest. (The parish ministry, which involves a great deal of personal counselling, visiting the sick, and so forth, is certainly a form of social work.) His transition, however painful or courageous it may be, is not without its material rewards. The ex-priest usually finds himself better paid, freer, more respected in the larger community beyond the Church, and faced with broader employment opportunities, once he has exchanged his clerical status for a professional lay position. (An employment agency specializing in ex-religious claims that average starting salary is $13,500 per year.[15]) These rewards probably do not account for very many clerical departures, but they do temper the image of the totally dedicated individual merely seeking a better way to meet human needs.

The idea that the priest serves these needs better outside the Church than in it has become a cliché of radical Catholicism. It is the equivalent of the conservative myth that all priests are highly dedicated, selfless individuals. One former priest insists that he would return only to a "new ministry . . . based on the principle of real service to real people. I can no longer genuflect before abstractions." Apparently finding the numbers on the Big Board flesh-and-blood enough, he lists himself as employed by a stock-broker.[16] Another former priest, who met his wife, a former nun, while both were working in a slum parish, says they would not return to the Church unless fundamental changes were made. They had found their inner-city ministry frustrating because of the attitude of their superiors, but he has apparently found more understanding guidance on Wall Street. He sells mutual funds.[17] (The stock market seems to be a common refuge for former priests rebelling at the crassness of the Church. At least one of the dissident Washington priests of 1968 has become a broker.[18]) The epitome of this particular form of altruistic secularity has been reached by a former Brooklyn priest, who was thwarted in his inner-city parish but found a way to "serve man" by writing cigarette commercials on Madison Avenue.[19] Later his poetry was published with illustrations by Corita Kent (formerly Sister Corita).

Father Gregory Baum, generally quite sympathetic to former religious, observes that some whom he knows, who left the ministry because they were disenchanted with the compromises demanded of them, have settled into worldly positions requiring even greater compromises and offering less scope for prophetic action. As heads of families, however, they can only accept their situations.[20] There is nothing surprising in this fact, nor does it cast any particular opprobrium on those caught in this way. (It does, however, suggest their naïveté about the world they chose to embrace so fully and casts a few shadows on their original decision to leave the religious life.) It is also not surprising that some quite blatant hypocrisy emanates from the ranks of radical ex-priests; they are as human as bishops. It is a more serious matter that so little attention has been paid to these phenomena in radical Catholic circles. The cause has been rather served by perpetuating, with half-conscious deception, the myth of the saintly ex-priest. That myth has by now received the official accolade of recognition from mainstream American culture—a *Time* cover story, in which it is predicted that within a few years all creative and intelligent religious will have departed their orders. Characteristically, *Time* finds among the more "fulfilled" ex-religious a former nun who is an editor of *Glamor* magazine, and a former missionary priest, married to a former nun, who sells insurance and mutual funds and insists he thereby "helps people" far better than he did in the slums of Peru.[21]

Most former religious seem to want to work out their salvations in their own way, and they have a right to their privacy. But a considerable number have also assumed a public identity and have raised questions about their old lives and their new ones which have become public issues. It is necessary, therefore, to ask what kind of lives ex-religious seek and what kind they have found. Most appear to be seeking a life of normalcy, as American society understands it. There is little reason to suppose that they are superior to their brethren left behind. In 1969 a nationally broadcast television program was devoted to the priestly crisis. One former missionary, who was married to a former nun, talked of how he had found meaning in marriage, a secular career, and an unstructured ministry. Afterwards he was shown entering his split-level house on a treeless street in a new Midwestern suburb. Another ex-priest described how he had become "more fully human" in spending six months looking for an apartment. For many the validation of "the world" is simply the canonization of the banal, the exaltation of liberal middle-class American values, although one of the main points of the radical critique of the Church is precisely the ease with which the Church has come to terms with society. There is no reason to suppose that departing religious will on the whole be any more immune to this tendency than those who remain.

Curiously, those who advocate a prophetic stance for the Church on great social questions often advocate gross conformism with regard to other things. Certain radical laymen welcome the news of priests leaving the ministry to marry. They resent the priest who is unlike themselves—through celibacy, or clerical dress—

and they look towards a great levelling which will obliterate these distinctions. They are also unsympathetic to the radical strangeness of the religious life within American culture, and when a religious leaves the cloister to marry they see it as a daring refusal to conform instead of an acquiescence in prevailing American notions about mental health, personal happiness, and a useful life. Predictably, some radicals are not content to advocate the legitimacy of clerical marriage; they now assert its superiority. One former priest, married to a former nun, says that those who marry seek to follow Christ more perfectly. He sees value in the celibate life because "when it is lived fully . . . it actually brings one to the point where marriage can be fully known as even more 'perfect' community life." [22]

There are compelling arguments on behalf of optional clerical marriage in the Church, but the movement against celibacy suffers from a failure to acknowledge the fullest implications of the question and from grandiose and unreal claims made on behalf of marriage. (An organization calling itself by the impressive title National Association for Pastoral Renewal seems merely to be a lobbying group against celibacy, as though marriage alone would constitute renewal.) There is no inherent reason why marriage cannot be compatible with the priesthood as it has been traditionally understood in the Church. (Certainly, marriage and a sacramental priesthood co-exist in the Eastern Orthodox churches.)

When the suggestion was first made that priests and religious should wear secular clothes, this was usually defended on the ground either that the religious life is a spiritual reality which does not depend on external signs or that clerical dress inhibits the religious in his apostolic work by creating a barrier between himself and those he seeks to reach. But it is now clear that many people who advocate abolishing religious dress in fact have a much more radical idea in mind—the virtual obliteration of any distinction between clerical and lay, a denial of the religious life as such and of the sacramental priesthood. (In 1970 the Dutch Pastoral Council demanded immediate permission for clerical marriage. The progressive Dutch bishops, who undertook to raise this issue at Rome, nevertheless noted that the council's document made no mention of the special consecration of priests, apostolic succession, or the sacramental character of the priesthood.[23]) Is it unreasonable to suspect that for some people the campaign against celibacy is simply the entering wedge of a campaign against the priesthood itself, as it has been traditionally understood in the Church? If so, are not many reformers precluded from supporting clerical marriage, whatever its intrinsic merits? (The Society of Priests for a Free Ministry is conducting a national campaign to re-admit married priests to active service. Yet its president, the former Jesuit Eugene Bianchi, elsewhere disclaims having "a superstitious hangup about having undergone an ordination ceremony," [24] a form of emancipation which is naturally not publicized in connection with the society's campaign.)

There is no more pathetic symptom of the Church's general sickness than the uncertainty of many religious concerning the nature of their own vocations. The causes of their uncertainty are easy to comprehend; they undoubtedly originate in a highly inadequate system of spiritual formation which prevailed until the Council and still apparently prevails in many places. The great terrible secret unmasked in the post-conciliar Church is the almost total absence of interior religious life on the part of large numbers of Catholics, including priests and religious. Their faith was wholly dependent on external support, and when this crumbled their faith crumbled also. To the question now so often asked, which apparently troubles so many sincere religious, what is the priest's task in the world?, there is an audaciously simple answer: to teach men to pray. The simplicity of the answer, and its obviousness, do not insure its acceptability. Many religious apparently see little value in prayer of any kind; they were presumably never taught to pray. (One former nun, who claims to speak for 240 ex-religious, says virtually none of them would defend the practice of meditation and most regard it as "an obstacle to the leading of a Christian life." [25])

The Church is presently crumbling not because its teachings are incredible, or because its structure is outmoded, or even primarily because of its moral hypocrisies, but because of the massive failure of so many individuals, including many anointed spiritual leaders, to interiorize their faith in a perceptible and authentic way. While the Church has need of learned priests, and humanly sensitive priests, and politically courageous priests, it has above all a need for holy priests, for which none of these things can be a substitute.

Radical Catholics who believe they are growing into a new maturity often cling to their adolescence in one important respect —they tend to blame their own failures on the structure or on their superiors; they take responsibility for their strengths but not for their weaknesses. Thus religious who admit finding no value in prayer do not often seem very concerned about this fact. Since the older piety, as they were formed in it, failed to awaken the spirit of contemplation in them, they feel no particular obligation to pursue the matter further. There is also no strong indication that the newer methods of religious formation are more successful in infusing this spirit. The single greatest failure of post-conciliar renewal has been the failure to revive the spiritual life, and this is more depressingly evident among religious than among laymen. One kind of progressivism now seems to ignore prayer altogether, at least as an explicit, distinctive activity. Michael Novak, visiting a convent of progressive nuns, finds there an uncritical acceptance of standard secular-liberal ideals and no vibrations from deep prayer life of a kind which occasionally can be sensed in older religious.[26] (Mr. Novak does not reflect on whether the kind of Catholicism he himself advocates might have contributed to this situation.) In 1969 a group of American bishops issued a letter on the status of nuns in which they said, "Although we cannot praise too highly those outsanding religious women who have concerned themselves with poor people . . . we must also recognize that these works . . . cannot dispense from the need of liturgical and private prayer." Sister Margaret Ellen Traxler, head of the 1500-member National Coalition of American Nuns, reacted quite defensively, insisting that "A sister is a human being and as such has . . . her inalienable right to follow the Spirit as she judges the Spirit to be calling her." Supporting this apparent claim that nuns have an inalienable right not to pray, Sister M. Claudia Zeller, Executive Director of the Conference of Major Superiors of Women, said, "I regret that a statement of this nature has emanated from the bishops' conference."[27] Curiously, Corita Kent, after contributing so much to the new, activist style of convent living in the 1960's, now states that she left the convent because it was too hectic and afforded little opportunity for contemplation.[28] Apparently, institutions will always be wrong, no matter what they do.

The Church needs to purge itself of oppressive and distasteful forms of clericalism. But if the price of this is the virtual disappearance of the religious life, or if the religious life cannot be successfully renewed, then the Church itself will simply perish. For some radicals this is the whole idea.

Notes

1. Sister M. Charles Borromeo Muckenhirn (ed.), *The New Nuns* (New York, 1967), p. 52.

2. Callahan, *Mind of the Catholic Layman* (New York, 1963), pp. 127-8.

3. Reported by Adolph Schalk, *U.S. Catholic and Jubilee,* July, 1969, pp. 27-36.

4. *National Catholic Reporter,* Oct. 16, 1970, p. 9.

5. *Commonweal,* March 15, 1968, p. 715.

6. *The Critic,* Oct.-Nov., 1967, p. 23.

7. Quoted by Walter E. Houghton, *The Victorian Frame of Mind* (New Haven, 1957), p. 259n.

8. James Colaianni (ed.), *Married Priests, Married Nuns* (New York, 1968), pp. 7-8.

9. *Commonweal,* June 20, 1969, pp. 392-3.

10. *The Catholic World,* Sept., 1969, pp. 251-5.

11. For Schallert, see the *New York Times,* April 26, 1970, p. 9E. For Gill, see the report by Andrew Greeley, *St. Louis Review,* April 3, 1970, p. 11.

12. *St. Louis Review,* Sept. 26, 1969, p. 12.

13. John A. O'Brien (ed.), *Why Priests Leave* (New York, 1969), pp. 35-47.

14. *McCalls,* Sept., 1970, p. 70.

15. *National Catholic Reporter,* April 17, 1970, p. 1.

16. Colaianni, *Married Priests*, pp. 2, 11.

17. *Ibid.*, pp. 14-22, 40.

18. *St. Louis Review*, Jan. 9, 1970, p. 2.

19. *New York Times*, Dec. 24, 1967, III, p. 13.

20. *St. Louis Review*, Feb. 6, 1970, p. 14.

21. *Time*, Feb. 23, 1970, pp. 51-8.

22. *The Catholic World*, Dec., 1969, pp. 112-3.

23. Reported by Frederick Franck, *Commonweal*, Feb. 6, 1970, p. 503.

24. *National Catholic Reporter*, Aug. 21, 1970, 2, 5; *Commonweal*, Jan. 23, 1970, p. 450.

25. Cited by Thomas Dubay, S.M., *Review for Religious*, Jan., 1970, pp. 114-5.

26. *Commonweal*, Sept. 5, 1969, pp. 540-2.

27. *St. Louis Review*, Dec. 19, 1969, p. 2.

28. *St. Louis Post-Dispatch*, Jan. 15, 1971, pp. 4f.

4.

Who Are the People of God?

EVERY high-school student learning civics or history is in-
noculated against the term "the people" as it is used in politics;
it is an incantatory word embodying only the vaguest meaning,
and it is misused sincerely by inept thinkers and deliberately
by demagogic politicians. Catholics in America have obviously
not yet reached a state of ecclesiastical sophistication comparable
to the average citizen's political sophistication; "the faithful" or
"the people" are regularly invoked by conservatives, reformers,
and radicals with virtually no effort to discover precisely who
the faithful are. Most bishops and religious revolutionaries probably do not wish to know who the faithful are, since precise
definition would rob the term of its authoritarian usefulness. In
the past, the hierarchy has generally been justified in assuming
that on religious questions at least "the faithful" were a unanimous and predictable collection; clearly, this is no longer the
case. However, it is probable that the masses of believing Catholics
are still much closer to the bishops on most questions than to
radical theologians and laymen. Radicals are consequently guilty
of the greater dishonesty in their willful ignorance about the
masses.

The conservatism of most laity, which dawned on reformers
only rather slowly, has posed a fundamental dilemma for the
whole reform movement. For if the imposed, elitist authority

97

of the hierarchy is to be repudiated, it must somehow be repudiated for the sake of greater freedom. Yet Catholic revolutionaries, like secular revolutionaries, have discovered that the desires and "felt needs" of "the people" by no means always correspond to the programs of the reformers.

Some radicals resolve the dilemma by blinding themselves to the emptiness of their talk about "community" and "people." William DuBay insists that there should be no speaking on the part of the Church except through the consensus of the people gathered in each parish. Yet the book in which he makes this assertion is a sustained polemic against precisely the consensus which does exist in most parishes, which the author believes is anti-Christian. His plea for lay autonomy and consensus is coupled with strong, dogmatic prescriptions for change, which the majority of laymen would probably find deeply repugnant.[1] At the 1969 meeting of the American bishops a young layman burst into the meeting hall and accused the bishops of moving in a totally opposite direction from the Holy Spirit and "the people of God,"[2] yet every survey of American public opinion indicates that "the people" are deeply antagonistic to precisely such disruptive behavior. Rosemary Ruether dismisses a book which is too much a matter of "Cardinal Suenens versus the Curia for the sake of rescuing the pope, and that is just not where most of us are these days,"[3] thus giving an interesting glimpse of Professor Ruether's conception of "us." Many radicals are simply insensitive to the attitudes of the masses and do not even realize when they are being offensive. Sally Cunneen, a lay editor, gives bishops the laudable advice to listen to their people occasionally. But without apparently recognizing the irony, she implies that listening to the people will mean discovering that they are simply benighted bigots.[4]

Daniel Callahan has acknowledged that the masses no more desire the new Church than they did the old.[5] (In fact, they seem to desire it less.) This realization has produced in many religious reformers a contempt for the ordinary believer which is sometimes ferocious and which can scarcely be exaggerated. John O'Connor finds his fellow Catholics "a herd," "straying apathetically behind," and finds it difficult to love them.[6] (When Mr. O'Connor was dismissed as editor of a diocesan newspaper the blame was laid on the authoritarianism of his bishop; there was no mention of his lack of respect for the readers he was presumably serving.) Father Eugene Schallert believes most Catholics have "a real gimmick"—maximum value (heaven) for minimum service. The Church is their "security blanket," and they care only about rigid formulas, not a deeper reality.[7] Anselm Atkins speaks of 500,000,000 Catholics, happy in their "folk religion" and "medievalism," and finds the ordinary believer a "superstitious religious caterpillar."[8] Donald Cutler, a non-Catholic religious editor, speaks of "the blindness of the hooked membership" (of the churches).[9] Father Gerard Sloyan applies to the Catholic laity the Duke of Wellington's famous remark about his own troops, "They may not scare the enemy, but by God they scare me."[10]

These remarks demonstrate an extreme readiness to judge and condemn, the kind of lofty censoriousness which progressives find deeply offensive in bishops. Yet their import lies deeper than a simple disregard for Christian charity. Attitudes like these have informed *aggiornamento* from the beginning. Re-

99

formers have had for the most part not the slightest respect for the masses, and their formula for change has been entirely elitist, the imposing of reform from above by an enlightened few. Rocco Caporale, a Jesuit sociologist, recounts his visit to a gathering of conservative laymen and how he had three hours to "turn them into a progressive group." [11] In general this has been the conception of religious change favored by too many reformers. They allowed themselves a few years to change the minds of the hierarchy and the masses and, disappointed in their lack of success, they came to despise those whose docility was insufficient. (Although progressives are scandalized by the paternalism that missionaries sometimes show towards non Westerners, it is apparently permissible for progressives to impose their theology on ignorant natives. Father Vincent Donovan, a Holy Ghost father in Africa, relates how a would-be convert who professes personal salvation or heaven as his motive is denied baptism "to prevent a distorted meaning of Christianity from creeping into the community right from the start." [12] Gary McEoin, a radical lay journalist, reports that the religion of the Brazilian peasants is largely superstitious and based on a false understanding of the sacraments.[13] Whatever the merits of these positions, they demonstrate that some people in the Church, despite their progressivism, still relegate to themselves the right to judge orthodoxy.)

Ecumenical advances also have taken place not only without the participation or approval of the officers of the various denominations but without the knowledge or consent of the majority of believing Christians. There is perhaps some value in the fact that relatively small groups of intellectuals discover among themselves that no important differences divide them, that the ecumenical age is in fact over. But what significance does this fact have for Christianity as a whole? In the minds of the concerned intellectuals ecumenism is apparently a dead issue, but ironically they are here being profoundly anti-ecumenical in that they willfully cut themselves off from the majority of believers for whom these same issues are by no means settled and who, if consulted, would probably not approve the way in which the new consensus was arrived at. Most radical Catholics seem to have solved the denominational problem to their own satisfaction and they have no respect for those who hesitate to accept their solutions. While struggling to erase sectarian differences of long standing, the radical ecumenist simply creates new sects within his own denomination. The bitterness attendant on this effort exceeds even the old bitterness between denominations. Ironically, many Catholics who profess to be scandalized over Christians worshipping as separate sects on Sunday morning and refusing to share each other's communion, disdain to take communion in their own parish churches and find it impossible to pray with their immediate neighbors and co-religionists.

Robert McAfee Brown has written, "I have seen too many people I love being crushed and destroyed by the slowness of present reform to be willing to settle for anything save the speediest of attempts to overhaul the church before all of them have to leave to preserve their integrity and wholeness." [14] Unquestionably, many sincere and dedicated people have been hurt by the failures of the churches in this age of multiple crises. Yet Professor Brown's lament reveals again the elitism of the reformers, their assumption that their own needs, their own sensibilities, their own insights have a priority and a superiority which the church must recognize. Yet it is probable that the uneducated,

101

devout, faithfully laboring masses of believers have suffered far more than have the progressives in this post-conciliar age. Much of what was meaningful to them in religion was abruptly and forcefully taken from them. Men whom they trusted appear to have betrayed them. The reformers have demonstrated little sympathy for the faith of the masses and have in effect waged a massive war against this faith. On thousands of occasions in the past decade, in many kinds of words and actions, the masses have been told that they are ignorant, superstitious, and unchristian. As Martin Marty has said, "someday someone will have to repent for a generation's neglect of the people caught up by forces of reform and renewal." [15]

Religious renewal since the Council has been on one level a frank snobbery in which the well-educated, articulate, relatively young have unquestioningly assumed their own moral, religious, and human superiority over the silent majority. An elderly widow disturbed over the suppression of novena services in her parish is at best patronized, and is often told she has no choice but to update her piety. But a thirtyish, college-educated, married woman who, despite the fact that she uses contraceptives, feels oppressed by *Humanae Vitae* is in progressive circles regarded as deserving of the deepest sympathy. When progressives speak of the Church's insensitivity to human needs and its rigidity they mean exclusively its insensitivity to their own needs, or perhaps to the needs of blacks and students (although blacks frequently deny that middle-class liberals are able to understand their needs). They show little evidence of broad human sympathy and often manifest the classic liberal syndrome—professed love for "people" and an inability to relate to immediate neighbors. The masses in the Church are assumed to have emotional needs which are in principle invalid, and the reformer's prescription for them is simply conversion. (Evidence of the progressives' confusion on this question was provided in 1970 by the controversy surrounding the purchase of the national *Register,* a moderate publication, by the right-wing *Twin Circle.* A liberal lay organization asked that the sale be halted until "the will of the people of God" could be ascertained and warned that the projected transformation of the *Register* into a conservative paper would cause "unparalleled division among lay and religious leaders." *Commonweal* worried that *Register* readers would soon be getting something "quite disagreeable—specifically the special political-religious doctrine of the Catholic Far Right . . . we may be in for even more radical polarization in the church in the U.S." The irony of the situation was the fact that the paper was being sold precisely because its circulation had dropped sharply when it was liberalized several years before, which was presumably an indication of popular will.[16] The implication of the liberals' complaint seemed to be that "polarization" could be prevented only by halting the spread of right-wing influence. *Commonweal* was simultaneously supporting numerous left-wing radical movements of various kinds without apparent concern over "polarization.")

Many of the older clergy seem in their day to have been much more successful in communicating with the masses in their own language than are the reformers. The older clergy were taken from the masses, and seminary education did not usually estrange them from the masses. Reformers rarely note the most impressive achievement of the older clergy—retaining the loyalty of the working classes, a task in which the more intellectual and progressive European clergy by their own admission failed. As Daniel Callahan has observed, prophets are often people who teach men how to make their peace with the coming generation,[17] and many spokesmen for radical Christianity can be seen as the heralds of a new class which believes it will inherit the earth, or at least the West—educated, articulate, liberal, flexible, upwardly mobile, professionalized individuals who recognize each other easily and are impatient that so much ecclesiastical power is still in the hands of backward, rigid, crude, amateurish clerics and laymen. The new class does deserve to assume some of the direction of the Church at this point in history, and when it does there will probably be improvements in many aspects of Church life. Yet the new class is appallingly insensitive to many of its characteristic failings and distressingly prone to identifying its own ascendancy with the coming of the Kingdom.

Michael Novak, who at one time saw the significance of popular Catholicism, later felt called upon to reject those church members who seek "a tidy cosmic picture in which they will find their place and learn what is expected of them." The Church, he argued, must increasingly disappoint such people. Father Richard McBrien thinks that the Church must not only be content to lose members, but must be willing to actively promote the disaffection of some people, and he does not hesitate to refer to wheat and chaff, although admitting that not all the latter will be rooted out in one lifetime.[18]

If these remarks seem to hint at something like an open purge of the unprogressive, others are remarkably explicit about their intentions. Rosemary Ruether writes,

Here the Gospel is indeed a sword, sharply setting off those who have ears to hear from those who will not hear. The irony of it is that the local churches are generally in the possession of the hard-hearted who bar the doors of the meeting-places against the agapaic community and . . . "even count it a service to God if they kill them." Consequently, the "true Church" perforce gathers for prayer in fields and streets . . . gathering the children of light and repelling the children of darkness. Such phrases . . . may seem pretentious, and yet those of us who . . . experience the crisis that is generated by the Gospel, cannot doubt that . . . the separating out of members of the congregation which . . . were unwilling to grow . . . expresses the same phenomenon for which the Scripture uses these phrases . . . [Those who leave] to seek the former religious security elsewhere are a real source of sorrow to the new community. They are torn between fidelity to Gospel, requiring going farther and faster, and responsibility to brethren.[19]

When the reformers see themselves as the modern equivalents of the apostles, and the conservatives as the false brethren, there is of course no possibility of simple communication, much less love, within the Church. Such parallels are often drawn by people who in other contexts insist that no conflict is possible between love of God and love of neighbor, that indeed the two are the same. They are sometimes drawn also by ecumenists who cannot bear the separation which exists between the denominations and think of themselves as heralds of reconciliation. Why should the laity take seriously the talk about freedom and consensus in the Church when almost the whole of *aggiornamento* has been elitist and imposed from the beginning? Why should they trust reformers who show so little respect for the masses and so little interest in their needs, who indeed become angry and condemnatory when the masses fail to live up to reformist expectations? (Monsignor Charles O. Rice suggests that a substantial segment of the Catholic rank and file should be allowed to drop out of the Church, because they are "racially bigoted and militaristic" and because "Catholicism has not been making much of an impression on them." Condescendingly, he admits that "one has to have compassion for all, even the bigoted ordinary Catholic with his narrow outlook." [20])

A good deal of the mistrust, cynicism, and inarticulate resentment which seem to infect the Church at present probably comes from the conservative laity's well-founded suspicions that some of their own clergy secretly despise them and have in the past half-consciously deceived them. Sister Patricia Flinn, a Midwestern high-school teacher, professes her love for the students she teaches but also pities most of them. The values they cherish she sees as "an ugly parody of humanity that it would be blasphemous to call Christian." She is miffed that they will not accept her criticisms. One student says, about black people, "I don't feel guilty at all." [21] (Progressives routinely criticize the preconciliar Church for instilling guilt in people, which only the Church could absolve. But many reformers are just as determined to implant guilt feelings, albeit of a different kind, and often they want to dictate the conditions under which the guilt can be absolved, for example, through the proper "radical" attitudes.) Father John J. Hill, who was first president of the Association of Chicago Priests, wrote that the parish priest's duties, including visiting the sick and "counselling uptight people," are "unexciting and of only moderate importance. Parish life is Dullsville." So pleased was he with this characterization of parochial life that he repeated it a month later, adding the teaching of catechism and burying the dead as parts of "Dullsville" and insisting that the priest has the right to seek a more significant life outside the parish.[22] There is nothing to distinguish this mentality from that of the teacher in a ghetto school who "knows" in advance that her pupils "cannot learn." One wonders how much assistance Father Hill is able to give the "uptight" whom he seems to despise or by what warrant the works of mercy called counselling the doubtful, comforting the sorrowful, visiting the sick, and burying the dead have been declared unimportant for the priest.

Ironically, at a time when radicals call on the priest to dissolve all barriers between himself and his people, to become one with the laity who share his priesthood, some clergy are in grave danger of becoming a special caste wholly cut off from meaningful contact with the majority of their people. Some young clerics seek to avoid parish life. They dislike their parishioners, and the parishioners dislike and suspect them. At some future time the Church may indeed find it necessary to ordain laymen in each parish to serve parochial needs, precisely because the professional clergy are unable to communicate with their people or win their confidence. The ordination of married laymen, which progressives look to as a liberalizing development in the Church, could in fact emerge as a highly conservative policy on the part of the hierarchy.

The "Catholic Revolution" has in reality been two-pronged, with the prongs pointed in opposite directions. It is the revolt of the elite middle against the authoritarian hierarchy above and the ignorant masses below. As such it follows a classic revolutionary pattern, including the fact that the revolt masquerades as a spontaneous popular uprising, while concealing the fact that special groups will be its primary beneficiaries. This situation does not necessarily invalidate the revolution but it makes legitimate the question what the revolutionaries will do for "the people" if they succeed.

107

Debating with Daniel Callahan, Michael Novak once argued that despite its lack of sophistication and openness as compared with the Church in Europe, the American Catholic ghetto was "thriving and energetic . . . I would not like to see it imitate Europe," [23] and his characterization was correct. There was a remarkable vigor in pre-conciliar Catholic life, even if not the kind of vigor progressives desired. The intensity, even fanaticism of belief, the all-pervasiveness of Catholic customs, the heavy financial sacrifices for the sake of churches and schools, the unusually high number of religious vocations, all these things testified to a genuine Catholic life of some depth.

Without at first admitting it, reformers saw the destruction of this ghetto as one of their principal tasks. At first they concealed this goal from themselves by assuming that popular Catholicism was simply a function of clerical authoritarianism, and that the people themselves were unhappy and repressed, ready for liberation at the hands of reforming angels. Preconciliar progressives believed that exposure to good liturgy, Scripture readings, modern religious art, and sophisticated sermons would have an immense impact on the masses, who would enthusiastically throw off the old piety to the consternation of their pastors and bishops. Only gradually was the reformer forced to acknowledge that popular religion is a separable phenomenon from official religion and that he found both equally distasteful.

"Ghetto Catholicism" thus became a term of utter opprobrium, equatable with rank superstition and wholly foreign to the Gospel. James Colaianni says that "Ghettoism suffocates. It is just another jail man builds for himself to keep from becoming free," [24] and this observation is a commonplace of radicals and many reformers. However, in illustration of the principle that avant-garde Catholics usually misread the spirit of the times, the word "ghetto" was beginning to have favorable connotations among secular intellectuals at precisely the time religious intellectuals were eschewing it. Ecumenically minded Christians began to find surviving Jewish ghettoes appealing, and secular intellectuals began to deplore the disappearance of ethnic neighborhoods from the urban scene (for "ethnic neighborhood" read "ghetto"). Above all, the American black ghetto has become almost an object of veneration to some liberals, a center of vital folk life at a time when the rest of the nation is blandly homogenized.

Radical white Catholics generally find themselves quite respectful of black pride and the refusal of militant blacks to adopt white ways and equally respectful, at a greater distance, of American Indian myths and customs, African tribalism, Buddhist rituals, and so on. Priding themselves on their sophistication about social realities, they accept unquestioningly the anthropologists' assertion that no myth or custom is truly meaningless, that apparently "irrational" beliefs and practices must always be approached respectfully and docilely in order to discover their meaning. Many of these same radicals are highly sympathetic to the attempts of young people to establish communes and communal living, which is often indistinguishable from building a ghetto.

These same radicals are, however, wholly unable to appreciate, or even to tolerate, the folk religion of their fellow Catholics. (When Cesar Chavez, the leader of the California grape strike, went on a lengthy fast and displayed a large cross at his headquarters, a former priest quit his movement in disgust.[25]) Popular piety remains a large hangup for many supposedly emancipated Catholics; contact with its artifacts or its devotees often produces emotions of disgust and fear, and the radical is almost always supercilious, cynical, and condemnatory of it. Father Eugene Schallert presumes to state that pious old ladies take comfort from "the rigidity of the Church rather than their concept of God" and that, as we have already remarked, those who believe in the Real Presence do not care about deeper reality.[26] Father Gerard Sloyan presumes to know that "Thousands of families still troop from parking lot to pew five and eight times a Sunday to participate in—nothing."[27] (People who continue to participate in nothing are clearly mindless fools and deserve no more than they get.)

The open, tolerant, democratic spirit which was supposed to characterize Church renewal should have dictated a tactful abandonment of the old piety on the part of the reformers, along with at minimum a silent acceptance of it as a possibly valid way for other men. Instead liturgists who gained power often tried to suppress the old devotions totally and systematically, while those out of power waged a running propaganda war against them, whose fruit was largely resentment, confusion, and emptiness of spirit among those of conservative ways. The reformers' professed philosophy should itself have dictated that believers be allowed to adjust to liturgical change at their own pace and in their own way rather than simply being told that the old was abolished and the new established. Liturgical change was also carried out rather dishonestly by many reformers. Originally, they told conservatives that popular devotions were invalid because they were theologically unsound historical accretions, dating from the late Middle Ages, the Baroque era, or the Romantic nineteenth century, while the aim of liturgical change was to return as far as possible to the authentic worship of the early Church. Only gradually did many liturgists reveal that their true aim was to construct a liturgy in as thoroughly modern an idiom as possible and that they cared little about the liturgies of the early Church.

Human communities are highly subtle and complicated realities, built up over many generations and held together at the deepest level by shared values, shared symbolism, shared history and experiences which are often not consciously recognized and often also apparently irrational. Originally, reformers, decrying the ghetto and the mindlessness which it presumably bred in people, called for a religion which was brave and personal, not dependent on social supports or social pressures. At a certain point, however, they shifted their emphasis from individuality to community, a renewed search for group identity and shared values. The reformer discovered that he needed the same social supports and social encouragement which he despised in the masses. He began looking for communal spirit and like-minded companions. In fact, he began precisely to build a new ghetto for himself.

In the meantime, however, the reformer had succeeded, far beyond expectations, in destroying the cohesiveness, the spirit, and the distinctiveness of the older Catholic ghetto. As Garry Wills has noted,

Bingo, large families, fish on Friday, novenas . . . clouds of incense . . . car blessings . . . *Dies Irae* on All Souls . . . the sign of the cross before a foul shot . . . food-chiseling in Lent . . . tribal rites, superstitions . . . and, all of them, insignia of a community. These marks and rites were not so much altered, refined, elevated,

111

reformed, transfigured as—overnight—erased. This was a ghetto that had no one to say "Catholic is Beautiful" over it. Men rose up to change this world who did not love it—demented teachers, ready to improve a student's mind by destroying his body. Do we need a culture? Only if we need a community, however imperfect. Only if we need each other.[28]

There is no doubt that within this folk Catholicism there was a great deal which was narrow, superstitious, petty, even pernicious and anti-religious. But such is true of all human societies, and of all human beings. The drive to "purify" can become demonic, and it sometimes did among the self-appointed leaders of radical Church reform. They thought that they could exactly determine and decree the kind of religious community they wanted and exclude all elements which they deemed unworthy. Instead they discovered that as much of the cement was removed which had held the community together, the community simply collapsed and disintegrated in their hands. They had destroyed the old, but they had nothing nearly so powerful or so broadly meaningful to put in its place. Communities grow spontaneously and organically; they cannot be planned or willed. They often take generations to develop, but they can be destroyed quickly. By failing to respect the genuine folk culture which was so much a part of the traditional Church, by assuming a stance of Olympian judgment over the community of which they were themselves members, radical reformers succeeded merely in destroying all community, the good with the bad, the genuine with the fraudulent.

The death of this community has meant for a large number of people the death of their religious faith as well. For an even larger number, perhaps for almost everyone, it has meant a weakening of belief—a loss of certitude, a diminution of joy and serenity, an unaccustomed cynicism and vague spiritual malaise, an embarrassment about expressing beliefs. Some radicals insist that these facts merely indicate the rottenness of the Church and the insubstantial character of Catholic belief. But no human values exist in isolation or can be meaningfully affirmed in isolation. *Aggiornamento* itself became a powerful force only when it gained social supports, and even developed instruments of coercion, when reform-minded individuals could take encouragement from each other and from various communities concerned about change.

Michael Novak once quoted Dostoyevsky with approval, "When a man leaves the people he becomes an atheist," [29] and it is clear that many reformers, who despised the folk religion of their youth, are now much closer to this condition than they had ever anticipated.

Notes

1. DuBay, *The Human Church*, pp. 59, 98-105.
2. *National Catholic Reporter*, Nov. 19, 1969, p. 2.
3. *Ibid.*, June 5, 1970, p. 15.
4. *Commonweal*, May 1, 1970, pp. 164-5.
5. *Ibid.*, March 3, 1967, p. 622.
6. *America*, April 9, 1966, p. 483.
7. Colaianni, *Catholic Left*, pp. 97-9.
8. *Continuum*, Winter, 1968, p. 729.
9. *Commonweal*, Oct. 31, 1969, p. 156.
10. *Ibid.*, March 27, 1970, p. 59.
11. Quoted by Michael Novak, *Saturday Evening Post*, Dec. 28, 1968, p. 28.
12. *National Catholic Reporter*, Aug. 7, 1970, p. 18.
13. *St. Louis Review*, June 12, 1970, p. 11.

14. *Commonweal,* Nov. 14, 1969, p. 216.

15. *America,* Aug. 31, 1968, p. 124.

16. *National Catholic Reporter,* Aug. 21, 1970, p. 8; *Commonweal,* Aug. 21, 1970, p. 405.

17. *The Critic,* June-July, 1968, p. 16.

18. McBrien, *Do We Need the Church?,* pp. 15, 207; Novak, *A Time to Build* (New York, 1967), p. 36.

19. Ruether, *The Church Against Itself,* pp. 152, 154.

20. *The Catholic World,* July, 1970, p. 158.

21. *America,* Sept. 26, 1970, pp. 200-3.

22. *Worship,* Jan., 1970, p. 58; Dec., 1969, pp. 635-6.

23. *Commonweal,* May 13, 1960, p. 179.

24. Colaianni, *The Catholic Left,* p. 22.

25. Reported by Peter Matthiessen, *The New Yorker,* June 28, 1969, p. 71

26. Colaianni, *The Catholic Left,* pp. 98-9.

27. *Commonweal,* March 27, 1970, p. 60.

28. *Ibid.,* Nov. 14, 1969, p. 217.

29. *Ibid.,* July 6, 1962, p. 381.

5.

Traditions and Institutions

RADICAL Catholicism has developed from a projected antithesis between "persons" and "institutions" in which the Roman Church, representing pre-eminently the latter, is seen as basically unconcerned about people and consequently willing to inflict severe wounds on individuals who fail to conform. Many radicals proclaim their principal purpose as destroying, or at least drastically changing, the institutional Church, to allow free individuals to live as true Christians.

The obsessive concern with institutional authority which marks so much radical thought grows out of real and serious problems. But in another way the radicals' preoccupation with institutions is made necessary precisely by their lack of respect for the majority of believing persons. As reform has failed to arouse the general enthusiasm which reformers thought it deserved, and as it has failed to stimulate the deep and remarkable transformations which they expected, only a few reformers are prepared to admit their own elitist biases, the fact that where reform has failed this has often been because the reformer tried to impose changes which the masses simply did not want. Instead, in order to retain the myth that *aggiornamento* has been a great democratization of the Church, the reformer must insist that the hierarchy alone impedes change. Hence "institutions" can be blamed but not people.

The notion of "institution" which radicals employ is also a very impoverished concept. It seems to imply an Olympian, alien, authoritarian superstructure continuously imposing itself on individuals from above. On the contrary, the social sciences, as well as experience, suggest that it is extremely difficult and artificial to separate persons and institutions. There are often tensions between an individual and the institutions to which he belongs, but most often this tension is fundamentally between persons or groups of persons within the institutions, not between persons and an impersonal structure. In the Catholic Church this tension is at present roughly between progressives and conservatives, with the latter in the majority, and it is only by overlooking the personalities of the conservatives that progressives can see their problem as primarily lying with "the institution."

Institutions rarely develop, and even more rarely are they kept in existence, purely by authoritarian plan or coercive machinery. (Even the Nazi state under Hitler depended in significant ways on popular support.) Most men live their lives as members of interlocking institutions of all kinds, and the needs and desires of the members have a great affect in shaping the character of these institutions. Whatever their grievances, most people appear to feel comfortable with institutions and have a proprietary, and sometimes a filial, attitude towards them. Anti-institutionalism has little appeal to them, and they are likely to be less resentful of institutional authorities than of radicals who promise to deliver them from these authorities.

This human dimension of institutions has been almost completely ignored by Catholic radicals. When Daniel Callahan wrote that the Church should totally rethink all her fundamentals, "giving no thought for the possibility of an institutional disaster; that is irrelevant where truth is at stake,"[1] he did not reflect that "institutional disaster" cannot help but include many human disasters as well—the large numbers of Catholics whose lives, in various ways, have been linked with the Church and who therefore suffer the same dislocations the institution suffers.

The standard radical response to this criticism is made by Rosemary Ruether: "I am afraid there must be much more and deeper insecurity in the Church before a new security is gained, a security which is truly unshakable because it rests on God and not on human structures."[2] This is a defensible position, perhaps even a heroic one. But as reform has developed it has been too often a heroism prescribed for others—the reformer himself frequently thrives on insecurity and uncertainty and cannot abide stability and order; he is determined to create situations in which others are forced to live as he lives; he universalizes and imposes his own values. In times of rapid change some people seek security by clinging to the old. Others are secure, however, in an uncritical embrace of change itself as the only true certainty. Rarely does the radical question by what authority he can prescribe insecurity for his fellow Christians, or how he will recognize the security which rests on God rather than on human structures.

Since the Council, many conservatives have shown that they also possess a free faith, that as external warrant is removed from many of their values, as the authorities in fact discourage many of their beliefs, they are capable of resisting, of taking a principled stand dictated by inner conviction, even under some circumstances (as with the Catholic Traditionalist Movement) of rebelling against the hierarchy.

On the other hand, reformers also failed to sense the central

117

importance of institutions in their own lives—what they mistook for an autonomous, free commitment often involved institutional supports which were merely more subtle than those of the masses. The great irony of so many radicals has been the fact that their anger towards the Church, and their alienation from it, seems to increase precisely as the Church becomes weaker and her oppressive powers all but disappear. They found the institution livable, if nettlesome, before it had reformed. Now, when there is almost no way in which the pope or the bishops can impose their will on independent-minded laymen, these same radicals dwell obsessively on the "repressive character" of the institution. As the priest-sociologist Andrew Greeley has suggested, many such individuals seem to need an institution which they can simultaneously hate and lean on.[3] They demand to be treated as adults and to be freed from fatherly control, but often this freedom simply leads to deeper bitterness, uncertainty, and disorientation. For many the assault on the institution is perhaps primarily, if unconsciously, a test of the institution's solidity, and when it proves itself vulnerable the assailant himself suffers severe traumas. Many who leave the religious life, for example, seem to be prudently abandoning a sinking ship to look for a stronger institution somewhere else.

That the anti-institutionalism and anti-authoritarianism of the radicals should result finally in new forms of institution and authority should not be surprising to any but the most naïve romantics. History records the same phenomenon endlessly with respect to religious and political movements which promised to abolish tyranny and establish perfect freedom. Yet a good deal of contemporary radical thought is based on a dogma which is not even recognized as such, a highly dubious speculation which is taken as certainty—that the human race is undergoing a profound transformation which will eliminate the need for law, tradition, authority, and duty, that men of the future will live as totally spontaneous beings guided only by their own inner promptings and their concern for others and capable of freely willing and creating a world immensely superior to any yet seen. Montaigne's dictum, "He who plays the angel plays the beast," is crucially relevant here, for if this dream proves false it will result in moral and physical catastrophes of unimaginable proportions.

To some extent this dream has already been tested on a modest scale in the post-conciliar Church. Although this is still a transitional period, it has become obvious that the belief of many people that they could sustain their religious life outside the institution and traditions of the Church has proven illusory. One of the great human costs of radical reform has been the large number of individuals who have simply become cynical, disillusioned, and bitter, unable to relate any longer to the faith which they have inherited but even less able to find a new one. Some relive endlessly their psychic wars with the Church of their youth; others settle, disillusioned, into a blander and emptier life than the one they formerly knew—the ex-missionary who sells insurance, the former Christian Family Movement activist who now spends his evenings with television. This is by no means the whole story of *aggiornamento*, but it is a larger chapter than most reformers prefer to recognize.

The underground Church has been for many radicals the great hope, a way out of the dilemma between the institutional Church and total secularism. Since it is by definition an unorganized, quasi-secret, local phenomenon, it is difficult to evaluate its suc-

119

cesses and failures. But people speak of it less, and less enthusiastically, than they did a few years ago. There are indications that many groups, started with high hopes, have disintegrated; perhaps they were held together merely by the idea of doing something new, or by the members' common disaffection with the established Church, but little more. In some groups, as with all sects, factional quarreling developed which was even bitterer than the original grievances which drove the sectaries out of their parishes. Those groups still functioning have existed at most a few years; it is impossible to judge whether they will prove viable over an extended period, or will be capable of surviving the kinds of crises which the institutional Church has survived many times.

Yet even in the apparently successful underground communities developments have taken place contrary to what were the founders' original expectations. A perhaps not untypical odyssey of an underground churchman would be somewhat as follows: (1) While convinced of his totally orthodox Catholicism, the progressive sought in small groups the fellowship, advanced liturgy, and sophisticated homilies not available in his parish. (2) Soon certain "peripheral" Catholic doctrines like papal infallibility and the Virgin Birth seemed dubious, along with certain practices like private confession. The progressive was still convinced, however, of the fundamental Catholic truths. (3) He ceased to be Catholic in any identifiable sense. The Mass, the Real Presence, the Trinity, the ordained priesthood, all came to seem at best symbolic and archaic. The underground community began to include Protestants. (4) The reality of God came to be perplexing and, perhaps, ultimately unimportant. If he exists, God is encountered in fellow human beings. There is nothing specifically "religious" in reality. The underground group is now a community of concerned human beings, although a high proportion started out as committed church-members.

Not all underground groups have followed this pattern, nor are all fated to. The morphology described here, however, has been common enough to suggest that, whatever their value, these communities cannot substitute for the institutional Church. They will inevitably issue in beliefs and ways of life different from historic Catholicism (or most forms of historic Protestantism). For many persons the underground Church has perhaps served the function which the philosopher George Santayana described for Unitarianism, "a featherbed for falling Christians." This does not imply that members of the underground have suffered moral and spiritual degeneration but merely that the underground, without their fully knowing it, served principally to smooth their path from Catholicism to secularism, the process traditionally described as loss of faith. Before the Council an individual who was dissatisfied with the Church had to struggle, painfully and largely alone, to extricate himself psychologically and socially. At some point he had to face the fateful fact that he had rejected the Church and was now a secularist (for reasons unclear such persons seem to have only rarely become Protestants). The post-conciliar Church has provided, unintentionally, various kinds of social supports for persons similarly disaffected. The Catholic who withdrew from his parish to join an underground group could initially justify himself as more truly Catholic than his pastor, who was neglecting to implement the reforms of the Council. As his own position grew more radical than anything the Council had justified, he shifted his claim to state that his was the Church of the future, the Church becoming, or that

121

he was getting to the roots of real Christianity, which the established churches all obscured. Only gradually did many members of the underground realize that they had ceased to be Christians in any distinguishable sense, that their position was really enlightened humanism. But the underground Church had rendered this conversion relatively painless and almost imperceptible.

The underground Church will always encounter the same difficulty in sustaining itself that radical theologians encounter—if the larger authority of the traditional Church is essentially denied, then any belief which the radical chooses to keep will seem arbitrary and unreal. Logically, there may be no necessity for regarding Catholicism as a seamless web which must be accepted or rejected *in toto*. But psychologically it is extremely difficult (though not impossible) for individuals to pick and choose from its traditions, and to feel justified. What begins as a rejection of the parish, or of papal infallibility, quickly becomes a questioning of the sacraments, and from there the Resurrection, the divinity of Christ, and perhaps the existence of God. Most human beliefs, especially those which are apparently incredible, grow out of a living tradition and are preserved in part at least by a social context. When the individual severs his contact with the tradition, or cuts himself off from the social context, he often finds that the belief erodes quickly. George Hafner, a New Jersey priest, assumed leadership of a Catholic underground in 1966. The group professed its basic orthodoxy and justified itself on the ground that the bishop of the diocese was reactionary and impeded progress in the parishes. By 1968, however, Father Hafner had left the priesthood and reported that the group found guitar liturgies and bread-and-wine eucharists in living rooms no longer relevant. Social action alone seemed important.[4]

Any group, or any individual, which chooses to reject wholly the authority of tradition or law in religion, to question radically every received belief, to rest wholly on what is "meaningful" and "relevant," is almost predestined, in this age, to arrive at a point of total secularization. For reasons both good and bad, a lively sense of God's reality and of man's ability to relate to him in a direct and perceptible way can scarcely be sustained in this culture without the nourishment of traditional roots.

The underground Church is partly a process of spiritual suburbanization, in which the relatively well-educated, mobile, young, and progressive citizens of the Church conclude that the old institution is rickety, decaying, dirty, and unhealthy and decide that their own future and that of their children require a cleaner, newer, freer, more open place to live and grow. Like those who flee the actual city (many members of the underground are literal suburbanites as well), most of these spiritual migrants maintain that they were driven from the Church by intolerable conditions. They leave behind, in the older Church, those who have the least resources of education, energy, sophistication, and youth to repair and maintain the structure. The structure begins to decay even more rapidly than before the suburbs were built, and the process of suburbanization is revealed as a self-fulfilling prophecy. Meanwhile the suburbs develop their own problems; some of the houses are rather flimsy, and services are spotty.

Like most suburbanites, the spiritual migrant seems only rarely to feel any affection for the decaying city which once nourished him, or any obligation to it. He is usually contemptuous of those who continue living in it in an effort to preserve and revitalize it. He is convinced that many of these city-dwellers are themselves responsible for the city's decline, because they seem ignorant, provincial, apathetic, unprogressive, and morally rather dirty. They are also suspected of committing many religious crimes, and above all the spiritual suburbanite is grateful for having escaped the crimes which seem to him to be the essence of Church living. In his new religious suburb he is able to associate almost exclusively with persons like himself.

Like the modern suburbs which surround the old city, the underground Church has of course grown from the institutional Church and still depends on it in numerous ways which suburbanites prefer not to acknowledge. (In general, they seem convinced that their escape from the city is a testimony to their own wisdom and virtue.) The relationship often approaches being parasitic, as the radical extracts from the Church whatever he finds useful but rarely feels grateful to the source or acknowledges any obligation to it. ("Churchy" matters, even involving reform, are often now beneath the radical's notice.) In 1970 an ecumenical group of Bostonians, including Harvey Cox, held a "Mass" on the Orthodox Easter which included parts of the Catholic and Orthodox liturgies as well as other elements. Its purpose, however, was apparently not to commemorate and renew Christ's historical Resurrection but to celebrate life, peace, and human brotherhood. The Catholic philosopher Louis Dupré afterwards issued a caveat in which he suggested that this service in a sense lived off the traditional Mass in a parasitic way. Part of its drama, its emotional effectiveness, depended on meanings attributed to the rites by traditionalists but not shared by those reusing the symbols. This kind of appropriation, he warned, would eventually secularize these rites and symbols, deprive them of their inner meaning, and thus render them useless both to traditionalists and innovators.[5]

Much of the new liturgy, whether in or out of the official Church, has depended on precisely the residue of meaning left in symbols after centuries of use for particular, orthodox purposes. Much of the excitement of guitar Masses, living-room Masses, sport-shirted celebrants, readings from Eldridge Cleaver, coffee-and-donut Eucharists, and post-communion dancing has depended on the dramatic clash of the old and new, the unexpectedness of it all, the daring and the shock it has engendered. Those not raised in the tradition seem rarely to be impressed with such things, and it seems likely that after a decade of such practices, when they no longer shock anyone and when younger congregants no longer have any real grasp of what the symbols once meant, they will be totally stale and ineffective. (For many underground groups that process seems to have already taken place.) The reasons for this are obscure and difficult to comprehend, but one fact seems clear—man needs roots.

To whatever degree radicals retain religious beliefs—God, the unique importance of Christ, the special significance of the Eucharist—these are derived from their nurturing in the traditions of the Church which have been preserved, deepened, and strengthened by institutional means. There is no reason to suppose they would ever have come to these values by themselves, or through the medium of modern secular culture. It is therefore not only inherently improbable, but also insufficiently humble, for radicals to imply that after centuries of distortions by the Church they have at last discovered the true meaning of the Gospel.

It is also insufficient to argue that while the Church served a historic function in preserving Christianity, this purpose is now finished and the institution obsolete. Many individuals have found that their rejection of the Church has made all religious belief incredible to them. Radical Catholics who have not migrated into total unbelief cannot accurately assess to what degree their remaining beliefs are the result of the massive spiritual pull which the Church still exerts on them. Those who so facilely oppose the "institutional Church" to genuine religion again show their ignorance of the true nature of institutions, which embody not simply bureaucracies, law codes, and buildings but also persons, beliefs, customs, art objects, and a whole fabric of human realities. The decline of the institutional Church has been accompanied by a proportionate decline of religious awareness on almost all levels. Catholics of all shades of opinion seem less sure of God's presence in their lives and less able to communicate with him. A too cavalier attitude towards traditions and towards the fabric of Catholic life seems largely responsible for this situation. Many Catholics are now suffering from a bad conscience about their past—they reject and detest it, yet it haunts them, and they feel guilty and disoriented as they try to flee it. Only when radicals have admitted the necessity of coming to terms with this past in a healthy, conscious way will the present spiritual sickness of the Church be overcome.

Radicals often respond to this apparent fact by arguing that it proves the corruption of the old Church, since if the pre-reformist faith had been truly healthy this decline would not have set in. But this proposition again depends on the very dubious radical assumption that man is on the verge of a new and higher state of consciousness, in which the traditions, institutions, and social fabrics which have been necessary in the past will no longer be necessary. If this day ever comes, it is not here yet. Radicalism itself—the ostensible reaching out for total freedom—depends on a variety of institutional and social supports, the most important of which are the respectability it enjoys in advanced intellectual circles (especially the strong pressures exerted by students and other young people) and the gathering of radicals into "communities" which often exclude non-radicals (hence the exodus from the parishes) and whose members constantly encourage and reinforce each other. If current fashions shift, as happens periodically, what are now unshaken radical beliefs will melt as rapidly as pre-conciliar Catholic piety.

Along with Orthodoxy and High Church Anglicanism, Roman Catholicism performs an important function in the total context of Christianity, that of affirming and progressively disclosing the corporate, hierarchical, sacramental form of belief which was for so long virtually the only form of Christian faith. The Roman Church will aid the other churches precisely by being true to itself, by continuing to witness to tradition and the various specific traditions not accessible in Protestantism. If Catholicism abandons this role as anchor to one side of the Christian spectrum, as modern Christianity's root to its older self, then Christianity as a whole will melt silently and almost imperceptibly into the secular world. This has already happened among Catholic and Protestant radicals who thought they had advanced beyond ecumenism.

When Father John G. Milhaven suggests that by the end of the century questions of absolute right and wrong will be mere curiosities, he also observes that the new morality may be an elite morality, proper only to intellectuals, while the majority of people may continue to understand moral obligations in legal terms.[6] This prediction may be too generous to intellectuals. Mankind has never yet attempted the experiment of sustained living without moral laws enjoying divine sanction of some kind. Public-opinion polls in America always show a large majority of people who believe in God, in an afterlife, and in moral law. More importantly, however, the absolutist morality of two millenniums of Christianity still serves as the foundation of Western ethical belief, however weak that foundation may now be, and Christianity is still the inescapable backdrop of Western culture, more than a mere memory. Radical intellectuals who reject this morality and this culture prove its continued strength by their inability to ignore it: they must continuously attack it and undermine it.

Moral and spiritual autonomy, of the kind radicals project as the wave of the future, may thus be an illusion. It is quite possible that the firmness, even the rigidity, of the Christian moral tradition simply provides the psychic security which allows radicals to engage in experimentation and iconoclasm. Since they know what the "absolute" is, even if they reject it, they can range freely through various kinds of negations, reversals, reinterpretations, and moderations, without losing sight of the core truth which the absolute law embodies. If the force of the absolute, of which the churches are the chief transmittors, is ever lost, this may begin an era of utter moral and spiritual agnosticism, of blind groping or total moral ignorance. (An example is the rejection, by some secular radicals, of the legal and sacramental institution of marriage, their claim that the bond of caring and loyalty between man and woman is alone important, not the formality of a ceremony or document. Yet it is perhaps only the massive insistence by society and the churches on the importance of the legal bond which focuses men's attention on the core of personal commitment which the bond is supposed to embody. A total abandonment of the legal bond might very quickly lead to an abandonment of the personalist ideal as well, and there is some evidence that such has already occured among secular cultural radicals.) Many individuals believe that their awareness of values originates with themselves and that they do not need authority, but this is often merely because they ignore their own childhood formations and the degree to which their supposedly freely chosen values were bred into them by an authoritarian background.

Almost all knowledge is socially constructed, in the sense that very few individuals possess the security and courage to continue affirming ideas and apprehensions which society continuously denies, even if these apprehensions seem very real to the individual. The decline of religious faith, of a sense of the reality of God, is therefore a necessary result of the decline of the institutional Church. For the Church is a numerous, venerable, visible, and respected community of persons who publicly affirm, in a variety of ways, beliefs which in this culture are inherently improbable—God and the whole dimension of transcendence. As the institution shows itself vulnerable, as the individuals within it show themselves uncertain and groping, as many of its leaders abandon it, the beliefs and values which it has specifically affirmed become increasingly incredible. Those who are indifferent to the fate of the institution are, knowingly or unknowingly, also indifferent to the fate of religious belief, of historic Christianity. A lively sense of the transcendent—the mystical awareness which radicals sometimes oppose to the institution—is not likely to survive long in individuals if there is no public institution affirming this possibility in the face of widespread social scepticism. (The most ardent anti-institutionalists now often admit that they no longer have a real prayer life or a sense of God and of Christ in their lives, although they sometimes assert that these things do not matter and are probably illusory.)

Radicals who reject the institution usually fail to acknowledge how quickly and how thoroughly their own dissent has become institutionalized and how much the credibility of their position depends on the existence of strong forms of social approval. In America at least the majority of articulate theologians, religious educators, interested and educated laymen, religious publishers and journalists operate within the limits of a semi-radical framework and, however much they disagree among themselves, they disagree with the traditionalist majority even more. Further, it is these Christians, and virtually they alone, who receive any sort of sympathetic recognition from the liberal, secular intellectual world. Traditionalist spokesmen cannot at present expect to be invited to conferences, subsidized by foundations, or publicized favorably in the most important organs of national opinion. Many of the radicals' prophecies are therefore self-fulfilling prophecies. When they affirm publicly that denominational differences are disappearing, that traditional dogmas are no longer important, that the institutional churches are in decline, and that a secular future is inevitable, they help to bring about these conditions, precisely because the general public, thus informed by the experts through prestigious institutions like *The New York Times,* assumes that it is must be true and begins adjusting accordingly. No contrary voices are raised from so nearly respectable sources.

Radicals tend to ignore the human costs of their programs, just as the old hierarchical leadership habitually ignored the human costs of keeping the Church peaceful and stable. Some of the casualties of change are conservatives, who feel shunted aside and unwanted, their most cherished values attacked or snatched from them. Another set of casualties, however, consists of those reformers who discovered that the more the Church changed the less they could believe in it and who ended with their beliefs and values in considerable disarray. When Father Gregory Baum offers examples of the new-style Catholic he mentions those whose marriages break up and who feel free to remarry, and those entering into mixed marriages who feel justified in having a Protestant ceremony.[7] On the surface these examples perhaps seem hopeful and progressive. Yet the human realities can sometimes be quite different—individuals willing to give up their children through divorce, ready to settle too easily on separation as the only solution, unwilling to look honestly at personal failings which undermined the marriage; others for whom their inherited faith has become a small flicker and who readily accede to the "ecumenical" requests of a stronger-minded partner. If the old legalism encouraged certain states of false consciousness—salvation through rote obedience—the new "humanism" produces its own dishonesties, like spiritual and moral flabbiness masking itself as a free open-mindedness. Some radical clergy and ethicians seem unwilling to take a principled stand on any matter pertaining to personal morality; those seeking guidance are merely told to follow their own consciences. But when the conscience is confused and agonized the individual is inevitably seeking something stronger, and it is probably a mistaken liberality not to offer some kind of judgment.

The importance of traditions and institutions in the Church is intimately related to the need to extend the Christian witness over time and space. Without institutionalization—of belief, of piety, of organization, of love—the Church can never be more than an ineffective, ephemeral reality. (Those who point to the early Church as an example of an unstructured community with a profound impact overlook evidences of institutionalism even in this Church and also the fact that as the impact of the Church became widespread, institutionalization occured quite rapidly. Those who point to the contemporary, highly personal Christian witness of individuals like the Berrigan brothers overlook the fact that this witness would have scarcely any impact on the American consciousness if the mass media did not choose to publicize it. It is impossible in the modern world to evade the need for institutions.)

The necessity of tradition, dogma, and institution in the Church can perhaps be demonstrated in a series of laws, relating to the preservation and dissemination of religious values in society: [8]

(1) Of its nature the Church is in tension between the transcendent values it seeks to manifest to the world and the worldly means it must use to accomplish its task.

(2) While the Church is always deficient in manifesting the divine reality to the world, it nonetheless gives this reality a minimum witness and a minimum persistence it would not otherwise have.

(3) The Church, whatever its failings in action, nonetheless propagates values and beliefs which will become real and forceful in the lives of some individuals.

(4) In every age and every culture men willingly seek to relate themselves to institutions embodying values and offering authoritative spiritual guidance.

(5) As the prestige of the institution declines, its prophetic and mystical functions will decline proportionately.

The fourth law is perhaps the crucial one; if radicals are

correct in their understanding of history this law is being abrogated. However, by the Iron Law of Oligarchies overt and explicit institutions are merely being replaced by subtler and often unacknowledged authorities which are potentially even more powerful. Those radicals who deny any substantial distinction between Christianity and concerned humanism perhaps evade the burden of the second law. However, if explicit religious belief is to maintain its existence in the world it will necessarily be through institutional means, among others. If the Church should be reduced to a mere collection of unstructured cells held together solely by personal feeling and commitment, historic Christianity would disappear in a few generations. Personal zeal inevitably wanes, and it is difficult for parents to transmit it to their children. Values which are not public, and which are not subscribed to by respected institutions, have a tendency to be lost. (Hence any incipient radicalism must always form itself into organizations and seek publicity or its thrust is lost.) A great deal of man's wisdom, and most of his values, are handed down by a rote process, and this insures their availability for those who may be prepared to internalize them and act on them. (Student rebels often maintain that their demands for social change are dictated by the rote teaching about "freedom" and "justice" instilled in them by their educations. To the extent that this is true it is an example of the third law.)

The existence of institutions also insures a comprehensiveness of values. All men's vision is fragmentary, and zealous adherents of whatever beliefs tend to be especially unbalanced in their perceptions. The institution of the Church, with its very rich heritage (the richest perhaps of any institution in the world), has preserved, however tenuously, a vast array of doctrines, perceptions, and amplified life styles which individuals from time to time discover and disinter. A powerful argument against radical theological change at this point in time is precisely the fact that severe historical pressures tend towards that end. What is reformulated now will necessarily be done hastily, with a sense of urgency after long delay, and under demands —political, ecclesio-political and so on—extrinsic to theology itself. What could easily result is a theology marvellously well suited to this particular age but severed from the historic continuity of the Church. Such a theology might well prove even less suitable for the twenty-first century than the rich tradition which now exists. (C. G. Jung explains religious dogma as the attempt of the Church to preserve and articulate great spiritual insights at a time when they are no longer deeply felt by individuals. To abandon dogma is therefore to abandon a treasure of these insights, in the arrogant assumption that men can acquire in their own experiences all the spiritual resources they will need in the future. Dogmas, and focuses of belief, tend to ebb and flow in popularity, and it is impossible to judge with any certainty what beliefs will be "relevant" to men of the next generation.)

Ironically, the radicals, in their attacks on hierarchical authority, have precisely shown the necessity of such authority for the Church albeit in greatly modified form from the past. The Church requires a principle of prudence and caution, even if historically this principle has been too powerful. If the charism and energy of the reformers had been allowed free reign after the Council, the Church would by now probably have been transformed beyond all recognition, and much of value would have been discarded. By their wariness and caution, the bishops and the mass of believers have served as a necessary check on radical imprudence. They have maintained a concern for those aspects of Catholic life which radicals do not care about, and hence in conjunction with the reformers, and in tension with them as well, they have insured a continued Catholic reality.

The institutional Church is the most economical and efficient means by which the Christian reality can be made accessible, at least minimally, to masses of people. Radicals who attack the institution are often aware of this fact, and anti-institutionalism is therefore often a different form of the radicals' elitism; it reflects their conviction that only a small number of people are true Christians and that no attention need be paid to the majority of professed believers. Any Church which attempts to relate to millions of people (ideally the whole human race) cannot help having rules and laws, dogmas and creeds, bureaucracies and treasuries. There are other aspects of this mass Church which radicals also do not recognize. Although the Church has been generally inadequate in terms of its social witness, it has maintained a genuine and necessary, though routine, concern for some of the needy through its institutions. This is no substitute for prophetic witness, but it is also not inconsiderable. When radical clerics and nuns now opt for an "unstructured ministry," in which the individual chooses to remain free of permanent institutional commitments in order to be available as special needs arise throughout society, they often do not seem to reflect that the institutions which the Church maintains—hospitals, schools, orphanages, nursing homes—require a dependable supply of committed individuals. Some of these institutions are now closing precisely because of this lack. When the radical cleric disdains this work he ought to ask himself the hard question to what extent his disdain is motivated by feelings of personal superiority over those who have performed these tasks in the past, or by a yearning for tasks which, while perhaps more challenging, are also more fashionable and glamorous than these traditional works of charity. The radical religious wants to move from university campus to inner-city to sensitivity training to whatever apostolate next becomes fashionable, and avoid the routine, boredom, and lack of recognition which characterizes hospital work or grammer-school teaching. Yet there is no reason for supposing that informal ministry to students, for example, is inherently more important than preparing elderly people for death.

The fifth law has already been discussed with respect to the concomitant decline of both the institutional Church and mystical-religious awareness since the Council. Many radicals, while rejecting the authority of the institution, nonetheless show their covert reliance on it in their demands that the hierarchy speak out against racism, the Vietnam War, and other issues. If this hierarchical authority is false, then episcopal silence should actually be welcomed as a further atrophying of this authority. Many radical clergy choose to wear clerical clothes, or identify themselves with their sacramental offices, only in connection with social protest. They use the prestige of the Church for prophetic purposes. But as the prestige of the Church declines, a decline they themselves have helped bring about, the usefulness of this tactic nearly vanishes. Ironically, the Church must maintain itself as a flourishing institution in order to project any significant moral or religious witness to the world. (There is a good deal more impact in criticisms of the Vietnam War by Paul VI than in the more vigorous pronouncements of the American Friends' Service Committee.)

Some radicals might conceivably grant the last four laws while seeking to deny the first. They would admit the importance of institutionalization, and of institutional witness, but then project a future etherealized institution free of all the petty, sordid, worldly, materialistic compromises the institutional Church has always engaged in. (On the other hand, many radicals do not at all mind financial concerns when these work in their favor. They often welcome the closing of parochial schools or the secularizing of Catholic universities, despite the fact that money needs alone usually dictate these policies.) This projection fails to take the world seriously, or the Incarnation, despite the radicals' professed attachment to both. Many progressives seem to find ecclesiastical fund-raising inherently distasteful, although they do not object to constant appeals, or high-pressure tactics, by secular charities or political groups of which they approve. They are scandalized by power in the Church, or by ambition and other personal failings in those who exercise this power. Often, however, they do not object at all to the ruthlessness of such men as Fidel Castro or various militant black leaders in America. "Confrontation" tactics are routinely justified when used by favored student or black radical groups. Apparently, for many reformers the Church is to be an angelic institution taking no thought for practical needs and never stooping to employ worldly means to attain its goals. Curiously, many of these same progressives are eloquent about the Church's need to embrace the world rather than stand above it, and to make itself relevant in a worldly way.

137

Notes

1. *Commonweal,* April 1, 1966, p. 55.

2. *The Christian Century,* Sept. 22, 1965, p. 1154.

3. *St. Louis Review,* March 13, 1970, p. 11.

4. Reported by Michael Novak, *Saturday Evening Post,* Dec. 28, 1968, p. 67.

5. *National Catholic Reporter,* June 19, 1970, p. 10.

6. *Commonweal,* Oct. 31, 1969, pp. 137, 140.

7. *Ibid.,* p. 127.

8. These laws are elaborated by the author in *Continuum,* Spring, 1968, pp. 60-71.

6.

The Discovery of the World

ALONG with "person," "freedom," and "change," one of the incantatory terms of radical post-conciliar Catholicism has been "secularization," the process by which religious believers allegedly lose their suspicions of "the world" and discover the necessity and desirability of accepting secular society in its own terms, as an autonomous reality not in need of a religious meaning imposed from without.

Radical conversions in thought and belief are never accomplished without mythologizing. Mere criticism of existing ideas can lead only to cynicism and disenchantment, and in order to replace one set of beliefs with another it is necessary to generate myths at least as powerful as those under attack. For Christian radicals the new mythology is that of "the world," an entity rarely defined with any degree of precision but ritualistically invoked as a justification for many kinds of new dogma.

In essence the myth of the world holds that Christians are spiritually separated from most human beings. While "humanity" struggles painfully but earnestly to build a world in which all men can live freely and without oppression, Christians avoid the struggle in the mistaken belief that their home is elsewhere—heaven—and that their religious duty is to prepare themselves for the afterlife, not concern themselves with contemporary problems and possibilities. "Religion" and "secularity" are thus opposed, and many Christian radicals have embraced a "religionless Christianity" which seeks to relate the Gospel to the world in an intimate and secular way.

On close analysis, this myth depends on certain implied propositions, the most important of which are these: (1) that mankind can be clearly divided between "religious" persons and "secularists"; (2) that religious believers generally have a strong sense of the impermanence of the world and of the reality of heaven; (3) that as a consequence they are unconcerned about the world and its problems; (4) that religious persons and secularists have widely divergent values and interests; (5) that in general secularists are more sensitive to contemporary problems than believers and more concerned to alleviate them.

Each of these propositions is at best dubious and largely fallacious.

(1) Taking the whole human race the proportion of genuine secularists, that is, those who strongly doubt the existence of unseen beings in the universe and their ability to influence human life, is quite small. Such non-believers can be found in appreciable numbers only in a relatively few areas of the globe— Western Europe and North America, primarily. The masses of human beings in Asia, Africa, and Latin America appear to be immersed in religious beliefs which are if anything pre-Christian, even as Western secularists proclaim a "post-Christian" age. Large numbers of American black people appear to believe in a Christianity which is really fundamentalist and pentecostal, and many important black leaders—like Martin Luther King—have preached from a firm religious context which enlightened secularists usually find embarrassing. Substantial numbers of radical young people now call themselves religious and profess belief in

astrology and other forms of magic. Secularized man exists, but he is much more a marginal phenomenon than his Christian admirers realize.

(2) Most religious persons, both now and in the past, have probably never had what could be called a "lively faith." Even in the Middle Ages men seem to have violated the Ten Commandments as freely as they do now, and rather than instilling in men the ability to live always for the Last Judgment the Church fostered an emergency complex, by which people generally lived in a quite worldly fashion and hoped to repent on their deathbeds.

(3) Crucial evidence for the radicals' criticism of their conservative brethren would be the phenomenon of large numbers of Christians living clearly unconcerned with the world. But such a phenomenon obviously does not exist. No less than other people, Christians seem to desire well-paid jobs, comfortable homes, and ample insurance policies, thus strongly discrediting the belief that they have their minds on the things of heaven. Individuals with deep religious convictions have shown an equally deep interest in worldly matters—severe Calvinists like the Rockefellers built the modern American corporation, and pious Catholics built the efficient political machines which dominated much of public life for so long.

(4) The assumption that religious people and secularists differ significantly in their attitudes towards the world is based on a special understanding of secularism. What the radical Christian seems to understand by the term "secularist" is the intellectual political activist. Many such persons are not secularists, however. Certain religious groups like the Jews and the Quakers seem to produce an unusually large proportion of progressives, but a substantial number can now be found in almost all major denomina-

tions. Many younger radicals would probably now deny that they are secularists; they are in fact much more credulous about the "supernatural" than most church members.

There is an overlooked class of secularists, however, who tend to vitiate the radicals' comparison. Just as there is a mass of ordinary believers in America, so there is a mass of ordinary non-believers also, individuals who have at most a nominal church affiliation, who rarely if ever attend church, who may even be hostile to or sceptical about religion, for whom religious beliefs are in no sense real or compelling. Since these persons are not organized they tend to remain anonymous, and their existence is overlooked in discussions about believers and secularists. There is no evidence that such persons are more socially conscious than believers; in general they probably share most of the attitudes of President Nixon's "silent majority."

(5) The fifth assumption depends on the validity of the fourth. Radical Christians have a tendency to ignore, in such leaders as Martin Luther King and Cesar Chavez, a piety and belief which appear to be quite traditional and which the radical ordinarily dismisses as outmoded and inauthentic. It is almost a radical dogma that traditional beliefs and traditional piety are incompatible with real social conscience, but the only sustained radical Catholic movement in America—Dorothy Day's Catholic Worker Movement—has been almost pre-conciliar in its orthodoxy, even in its respect for the hierarchy.

On balance the Catholic Church in America probably has a record of concern for social justice which is better than that of most institutions, although it is certainly not brilliant. Progressive attitudes on social questions can usually be correlated with education, family, and group traditions. Only educationally and economically rather elite groups like Quakers, Unitarians, and Reform Jews are conspicuously more liberal than Catholics. The Catholic Church is a mass movement, with attitudes which inevitably reflect the attitudes of the general society. The radicals' position on "religion" vs. "the world" rests on a profound and unrecognized contradiction. In general radicals have accepted, as part of their secularization, the idea that religion in no sense partakes of a "supernatural" reality, that ideas about God are wholly human constructs, that ethical norms evolve culturally, that direct contact with any superior being is not possible. If, however, religion is to be thus considered as a purely human creation, then it deserves the same interest and respect which radicals confer on all other forms of human creativity. Religion has been a universal phenomenon, in all times and all cultures. Whatever its origins, it has shown itself profoundly rooted in the human spirit and possessed of the most powerful and persistent resources in all manner of human situations. No person who professes respect for human creativity, or human beings, can afford to reject this phenomenon as essentially insignificant or pernicious. Yet Christian radicals often do precisely this. They are curiously at one with the ultra-orthodox in positing an almost complete distinction between "Church" and "world," although the orthodox urge a shunning of the world while the radicals are equally vehement on the need to shun the Church.

Religious who leave the cloister to find the "real world" seem rarely to reflect that the community they leave behind is just as real, and just as human, as the one they enter. It has been conceived by human minds, organized by human ingenuity, and kept going by human cares and ideals. It is no more invalid, or less "worldly," for certain individuals to choose to work out their

143

lives in the human communities known as convents than for others to live in inner-city ghettoes, suburban ghettoes, academic ghettoes, hippie ghettoes, small-town ghettoes, or any other of the innumerable limited communities men have always constructed for themselves. Radicals who oppose "religion" to "the world" seem to be making the unrecognized assumption that religion really is a supernatural intrusion into secular life, which must be shunned for that reason.

The radicals' idea of "the world" is, like so many of their most central ideas, highly elitist, and the radical mythology is understandable and consistent only when this elitist bias is recognized. At least through the decade of the 1960's, "the world" meant to radicals university campuses, black ghettoes, Latin American guerrilla enclaves, hippie communes, and underground religious communities but not, apparently, suburbia, St. Patrick's Cathedral, the White House under Johnson and Nixon, IBM, or the John Birch Society. Thus "the world" could be defined as essentially good, a highly promising and attractive place which religious traditionalists were incapable of appreciating. Those features of reality which were troublesome and unattractive were not included in the romantic image of "the world" which Christians were ceaselessly exhorted to admire and love. (By 1970 there were signs that radicals had begun to rediscover the Silent Majority and were about to readmit them into "the world.")

The blatant contradiction between so many repulsive features of modern life—war, poverty, the deterioration of the environment—and the goodness of "the world" has often been smoothed over in radical thought by making "the world" essentially a future thing, with only a tenuous existence in the present. The significance of the "theology of hope" and of the emphasis on "man becoming" is that these concepts provide strategies for avoiding the hard question of how blatant evil (to which radicals have been keenly sensitive) can be reconciled with the idea of the world as inherently good. "The world" is identified solely with those realities which seem progressive and future-oriented; most of the past and much of the present can then be dismissed as somehow unreal. For some radicals the future seems to be the spiritual and psychological equivalent of heaven—the projected perfect world which will blot out the misery of the present and which makes the present bearable. (Politicized radicals also see this future paradise as the time when the good will be rewarded and the evil punished.)

Most Christian radicals do not seem to love or understand the world. They may love, quite intensely, certain limited patches of it, as do most men. Above that they love an idea of the world, or a projection of how the world might be. But when lovers do not see each other in reality, when one loves chiefly an image of the other, or looks continuously to reform the other, emotional disaster results. The Christian radicals' love affair with the world may well have this same outcome.

Unwittingly, many religious progressives have proven their own unworldliness precisely in their concern to be worldly. It is by now almost a law that religious liberals will discover and espouse various aspects of American culture just as true secularists become disenchanted and begin looking for realities which the religious progressive is trying to forget. Thus progressives discovered, wonderingly, the cool detachment and academic rigor of the secular universities just before these schools erupted in fierce rebellion, as students demanded an education centered on values and related to personal beliefs. They admired the high quality of the public schools just before black parents began to accuse these same schools of cultural genocide, white high-school students rebelled, and a flood of studies appeared to claim the public schools as miserable failures. Catholic intellectuals began to endorse the disinterested honesty of the social sciences only a few years before a wave of reaction set in against these disciplines, whose "objectivity" was denounced by secular radicals as both fraudulent in practice and inhumane in theory. Priests and nuns began leaving the religious life to join social-welfare agencies at about the time the War on Poverty was generally conceded to have failed, and radicals were denouncing these agencies with as much vehemence as they denounced the churches. Daring clerics enthusiastically proposed psychiatry as universally relevant to the religious life just before some secularists began calling attention to the manipulative uses of psychiatry and radical young people refused to allow their own commitments to be psychologized away. Pre-conciliar liturgists insisted on a spare, clean style in religious art a few years before the explosion of pop-art, op-art, and neo-art-nouveau. Chic nuns started smoking as sensible laymen were quitting. Advanced clerics began quoting *Playboy* just before Women's Liberation revealed the inhumane, oppressive character of that publication.

In each case what is at issue is not whether the religious radical or the secular radical was more correct in his opinions, the former always a few paces behind the latter, but the fact that so many religious progressives seem to operate with no clear principle except that of trying vainly to keep up with the secular world. The religious reformer has often been left, in the decade past, earnestly endorsing ideas whose proponents were in the process of abandoning them. If nothing else the reformer often showed himself distressingly devoid of his own convictions and a highly unreliable guide through the ways of the world. As Daniel Callahan pointed out, Harvey Cox's influential secular-city concept caught the mood of the Kennedy years, while Rosemary Ruether's prescription for the Church was based on the civil-rights movement. Both phenomena were dead almost before these models could be placed before the religious public. Mr. Callahan continued,

It is bad enough trying to get straight on the shifting schools of biblical exegesis, church history, and systematic theology these days. When it is also necessary to get the secular culture straight at the same time, and then bring together everything in holy wedlock, nothing less than unbounded confusion is likely to result. And unbounded confusion is what we have, however much this befuddlement is given a halo and the confessedly uncertain man turned into the modern saint.[1]

The worldly naïveté of progressives has often also prevented them from perceiving elements of worldly wisdom within the religious tradition they are discarding. Thus James Colaianni writes, "The parish structure was ill-conceived in the first place . . . because you simply cannot geographically organize a city; it has been tried endlessly and has never worked."[2] Absent from this astonishing statement is any apparent awareness that for over a century much of America's urban political life was precisely organized, highly efficiently, on a geographic basis— the famous system of ward politics—and that this system still survives strongly in many places. The flight to the suburbs, to small autonomous communities, demonstrates precisely the desire of many people to live in geographic enclaves within the larger metropolis. Real-estate agents exploit, as an attraction, the

147

existence of parishes in newer suburbs, even to using parish names in their advertisements. Urban sociologists have long realized that quasi-autonomous neighborhoods are usually the backbone of flourishing cities, and the local parish is often in turn the backbone of the neighborhood.

Catholic liberals who formerly quoted the papal social encyclicals were often embarrassed by one feature of these writings—the "principle of subsidiarity," which held that no function should be performed by a higher institution (such as the national government) which could be performed effectively by a lower (such as the local government, or the family). Strong supporters of the New Deal and the welfare state, and beleaguered by "states' rights" advocates, liberals ignored this principle as much as possible or explained that in practice the lower institution was rarely capable of performing most functions effectively. Now, however, the New Left and the black militants have revived the substance of the principle of subsidiarity in their demands for "community control" and their antagonism to super-agencies of all kinds. Thoughtful liberals are also beginning to have misgivings. The Catholic liberal, by his inattention to an integral part of his own tradition, lost contact with a useful idea highly relevant to the present social situation. (Catholic secularists conversely also refuse to learn from the world when they find it inconvenient. Although every kind of secular movement—from General Motors to SDS—has found that full-time organizers are necessary for success, Catholic progressives dogmatically call for a part-time priesthood.)

Progressives who insist on their love of "humanity," and their desire not to reject anything human in the name of transcendence, are often driven from the Church precisely by its humanity. They

148

are shocked, angered, and finally embittered at the discovery that popes, parish priests, and ordinary laymen can be proud, dishonest, venal, and morally insensitive. They almost paraphrase St. Augustine, "Oh Lord, let me be human—but not yet," and they would apparently find the Church palatable only if it were composed exclusively of right-thinking, courageous, selfless individuals.

This rather odd concept of "humanity" points directly to the radicals' most fundamental disagreement with traditional Christianity, although this disagreement is only rarely made explicit. The Christian doctrine of man, which is even more extreme in classic Protestantism than in Catholicism, holds that human beings are by nature sinful, that to be human means to sin, and that sin is overcome only through divine grace. Modern Christian radicals, however, wish to equate "humanity" with some kind of perfection, so that by definition what is "truly human" is always good, true, and beautiful. When men behave immorally, as of course they commonly do, this immorality is somehow regarded as foreign to their humanity, although its existence within individual men is not often explained. Insofar as radicals do attempt to explain evil they seem to find it in culture and society—individual men, who left to themselves would always live morally and creatively, are deformed by social pressures of various kinds. Only under such assumptions can "human" be understood so positively as radicals now seem to understand it.

As further evidence of their curious tendency to misunderstand the secular world which they are so eager to know and love, religious radicals formulated this notion of a benign humanity progressing towards a higher state of being at precisely the moment when many secularists—of all political stripes—feel a cynicism and pessimism about "the world" comparable to the feelings Catholic radicals have about the Church. Conservatives believe society is rapidly deteriorating; liberals fear that necessary moderate reforms are being destroyed by the combined pressures of left and right; radicals believe society needs major surgery but is unwilling to undergo it. The "theology of hope" and the interpretations widely put on the theology of Teilhard de Chardin seem to be hangovers, in the American Church, of the facile optimism nourished by the Kennedy administration and the Second Vatican Council, when it appeared for a few years that amazing progress was being made towards the solution of all significant problems both secular and ecclesiastical. It was in these years that the secular-city theology arrived to sanctify cool, pragmatic, technocratic, urban American man, with Harvey Cox canonizing the style of life symbolized by John F. Kennedy just as Norman Vincent Peale had canonized the life style of Dwight D. Eisenhower. (With a curious myopia about his own religious tradition Michael Novak, while admitting that the secular-city theology was outdated almost before it appeared, defends it on the ground that it taught Christians not to fear the city but to embrace urbanity in all its aspects.[3] American Catholics, however, have always been urban people, have shown little affinity for the ideal of rural arcadia, and long ago mastered certain fundamental crafts of urban life, like ward politics. This is the kind of dirty, mundane urbanity that did not fit Harvey Cox's mythologized version and was therefore omitted. Five years after *The Secular City* appeared, intellectuals began once more to discover white working-class city-dwellers, whom Catholic intellectuals should have been aware of all along.)

The mood of disillusionment and despair which now affects

so many secular liberals and radicals is largely a moral hang-over which followed the intoxicated euphoria of the Kennedy era. Christians were uniquely situated to innoculate secularists against such a hangover, precisely through the awareness which their tradition imposed on them of the radical sinfulness of man, which is capable of poisoning the most promising dreams, and the unreliability and impermanence of all things human. Instead, however, too many Christian progressives chose to ignore this central insight of their tradition and to plunge uncritically into the secular-liberal dream of Camelot, gilded with various theo-logical decorations. The Christian who wished to be relevant to his culture missed the opportunity precisely through his infidelity to his religious heritage. Catholicism at present badly needs a theology of pessimism, a way of validating life in a world where defeats seem infinitely more common than victories, despite men's grand expectations. Instead the thrust of modern theology seems to be in the direction of a compulsory optimism (à la Teilhard de Chardin) which cannot help issuing in recurring despair and disillusionment.

The radical Christians' celebration of man-making-the-future and man-perfecting-his-world coincides almost exactly with the discovery of the ecology crisis. But the deepest implications of the ecology crisis are rarely noticed by these religious radicals. If in great part the crisis stems from man's wanton use of nature for his own narrow ends, then secular-city theology must be seen in part as a misguided celebration of precisely those attitudes which had brought on the crisis. The older theological traditions which were wary of science and man's manipulative possibilities, and inclined towards a religious awe of nature, may prove more useful to secularists of the future than the bright modernity of

151

Harvey Cox. Beyond this, however, it seems clear that the ecological crisis has resulted not simply from man's greedy and thoughtless exploitation of nature but has been largely the result of the best motives, the desire to make the world a more benign, healthy, and comfortable place. Each of these efforts, however, had unforeseen unhappy effects. Man can derive from this new crisis only a deepened humility, a renewed sense of his own finitude, radical doubts about his ability to foresee the future and plan and work for it rationally. For man to survive he may need much more of traditional religion's sense that he is a part of a larger cosmic process which he can only partially understand and control.

Lewis Mumford, a trenchant critic of technology and society, has pointed out a common modern fallacy—that decay always results from the dead hand of conservatism, when in reality cultures also decay when they break too rapidly and completely with the past. He adds: "For a culture like the present one to cultivate its transience and ephemerality, as if dynamism were an absolute value and stability of any kind a handicap, is to ignore the plain facts not only of organic continuity but of physical existence."[4] The deification of change which radical Catholicism has effected, and its utter lack of concern for the Catholic past, is in part a manifestation of a modern cultural sickness.

Many radicals seem not to have realized until very late that the crisis of the Church is merely part of a larger crisis of civilization; many now seem to realize it only dimly and not to give it sufficient weight. For a long time the Church was measured against the institutions of the world—the universities, the liberal democratic state, the public schools—and found to be miserably wanting in contrast to these enlightened, healthy realities. Only gradually were these secular realities revealed to be just as sick as the Church. The problems which plague Christians are in large measure the problems which plague modern Western man and they are not solved by abandoning the Church for "the world."

Almost inevitably many religious radicals who reject the authoritarian character of the Church, who deny that the Church represents any kind of ultimate or absolute, unconsciously find substitute authorities, surrogate absolutes, in the mythologized world which they are so eager to know and love. Robert Hassenger, a Notre Dame professor, sees as a "religious expression," substituting for conventional piety, the communal spirit of the Houston space team after a successful rocket blastoff.[5] (Shortly after this blessing was bestowed, many secular liberals began to feel grave misgivings about the validity of the entire space project.) Mary Daly virtually enthrones "youth" as a new magisterium defining truth and morality. Academic theology, she finds, is discredited because youthful realism "sees through" its "styles and games." Gregory Baum's emphasis on the uniqueness of Christ she calls into question because "Many college students . . . would have difficulty with it," and his attempts to reinterpret certain religious traditions would cause "the young" to say "So what?" The ordained priesthood, she believes, has no future, because "students" regard it as unimportant.[6] (Many radical Catholics are driven to endorse the youth culture and look for allies in it because it is the only substantial group whose attitudes are similar to their own. Even so, the conservatism of many college youth is greatly underestimated by these same radicals. They also make the curiously static assumption that youth is unchanging—what young people believe today is necessarily what they will believe in fifteen years.)

Rosemary Ruether, as a good ecumenist, disdains to draw boundaries between denominations, but she is prepared to draw a line between "those who are in the Resistance and those who are not." [7] thus absolutizing a political movement in a way she would refuse to absolutize any religious movement. Francis Carling, a sympathetic spokesman for the Catholic New Left, admits the phenomenon of students revolting against the rigid moralism of the Church but then embracing the rigid, manipulative ideology of radical political activism.[8] (The curiosity exemplified here—of Catholic radicals who despise fanaticism and coercion of all kinds in religion but welcome it in politics—is one of the most intriguing developments of the post-conciliar Church.) William DuBay says that blacks are going to convert "us" and force "us" to reform.[9] (In general, of course, radicals find religious and moral coercion unspeakably anti-Christian.) The British Catholic leftist Terry Eagleton insists that the Christian commitment requires a revolutionary political stance, "in the Marxist sense." [10]

Many Catholics who can no longer find meaning in the old piety have apparently discovered a substitute in "sensitivity training," the "basic encounter groups" by which individuals are alleged to discover the truth about themselves and their relationships to other people through intense, prolonged personal confrontations. When Andrew Greeley expressed strong reservations about the movement, he elicited sharp and defensive responses not dissimilar to those emanating in the past from devotees of Our Lady of Fatima. A Josephite priest insisted that only those who had never been involved in sensitivity training

154

would criticize it and wondered about the "suspicious, negative, cynical mentality" of Catholic critics. A Jesuit suggested that psychoanalysts criticized the movement only out of fear of losing paying patients. Another Jesuit imagined Father Greeley as "a lonely, terrified shooter on top of a watchtower, firing at random at the jungle down below . . ." A third Jesuit psychoanalyzed Father Greeley from his vantage point in the Caroline Islands and decided that the Chicago priest wanted to participate in the training groups but was fearful of what he would discover about himself. Greeley, he concluded, lacked a clear grasp of his own identity and had problems with a father figure. The sensitivity trainer, he insisted, never manipulates people and never plays the guru.[11] Catholics who discovered during *aggiornamento* that the Church no longer had all the answers have sometimes discovered the answers elsewhere, and like the preconciliar pious zealot they are sure that only personal faults of some kind prevent other people from seeing the same truth.

The progressive Catholic's love of "the world" does not insure that all progressives will love only what is best in the world. The secularizing theologies have justified for many people the relaxation of all tensions between themselves and their culture, between religion and profanity, and some have discovered that they can live easily, as enlightened modern Catholics, simply by doing what the world does. (Thus, as we have seen, the spate of ex-priests selling insurance and thereby finding a more significant human life than in the ministry.) Corita Kent finds beauty and religious significance in highway billboards and cheap commercial bread. Gerard A. Pottebaum and Joyce Winkel, two "catechetical experts," have composed a book, *1029 Private Prayers for Worldly Christians*, which attempts to

155

integrate prayer with advertising slogans. As Mr. Pottebaum explains, "The writers of the scriptures and the adman speak a common language. Both tell of man's thirst for a new life, to go 'where the flavor is.' We just get enough. We yearn to drink deep of the fount of life everlasing. Every bit seems to bring us closer to fulfillment—even a silly millimeter." The book, by combining biblical quotations and advertising slogans, "serves to remind the reader constantly that prayer is not removed from the everyday world." (That paragon of "worldliness," *The New Yorker,* saw fit to reprint the publisher's news release on the book as an example of unintended absurdity.[12])

If these things can be dismissed as the silly excesses bound to creep into any movement, it is nonetheless true that few Catholic radicals appear to have any principles, or any basic strategy, for dealing with the problem of drift—the process by which beliefs, ways of living, values change not through any reasoned argument or profound life experience but simply because the culture itself changes and the individual has no resources for resisting the tide, indeed has come to believe that such resistance is futile and unnecessary. For many progressive Catholics the problem has become especially acute, since without institutional support they now find themselves in moral and spiritual situations which they never consciously chose. They are no more free, in a moral sense, than they were in their orthodox days. The problem of drift will probably become especially acute in the generation ahead, among adolescents who will inherit a Catholicism devoid of almost all authority, passed on to them without conviction by parents whose own religion is quite vague. The force of the culture, and especially the youth culture, will be virtually irresistible in the lives of many individuals, who are not likely to be happier, freer, or more creative as a result.

The phenomenon of drift is curiously at odds with prevailing radical theologies, which proclaim man's ability to choose his future freely and to make his world. Many of those who espouse these theologies simultaneously act and talk as though human beings have no choice but to conform themselves to the flood of history. What appears to be the historical fact of the decline of religion in the West is taken by these radicals as necessarily normative—not only is the world becoming more secular, but this is inevitable and Christians must accommodate themselves to it. Yet if man truly controls his future, and is truly capable of making his world, then there should be no barrier to some men's willing and achieving the continuation of a sacral world, or a traditional world, or any other kind of world they may desire contrary to the secular idea of what is "progressive." It is doubtful if many religious radicals really believe in the freedom which they extol. They seem often to fear the world, and fear history, and they desire as a consequence to maneuver themselves into favorable positions relative to the world's movement, where they will not be steamrollered or left behind. Despite their cry for greater freedom in the Church they have swept many followers into their stream precisely by playing on this same fear of history, or by implying that men have no choice but to accept change as it occurs. Cynthia Wedel, the president of the National Council of Churches, says that social change is a clear sign of God's action and those who fear change lack faith.[13] This useful formula, which many radicals employ in a variety of ways, appears to give Christians no basis on which

157

to distinguish desirable from pernicious change and no grounds for suspecting that apparently beneficial changes may later reveal themselves as pernicious. A genuinely healthy attitude towards change would be one which permits the individual to accept or reject change as it seems good to him. To elevate change to a kind of absolute is suggestive of an unhealthy insecurity. (There is also an unrecognized dishonesty here—when the radical approves the prevailing course of society he appeals to "relevance" and "history." When the tide turns against him he shifts to "prophecy" and "witness.")

The chief criticism which can be directed at old-style Catholics is precisely the fact that they seem too worldly, that the force of other-worldly theology appears not to have intruded itself into their lives. But if the stringency of the old theology had such meager results, what can be expected from the looseness of the new? If in the new dispensation Catholics are exhorted to love the world and to find no tension between themselves and it, in the long run this is likely to lead to a totally uncritical and placid acceptance of everything which culture or the state makes normal. This is a problem to which radicals have addressed themselves only feebly. Anselm Atkins says, "Secularization is good for the Church when it means critical receptivity to scientific and intellectual discoveries, and bad when it means fraternization with money and repressive power." [14] Atkins does not attempt to defend this rather arbitrary distinction, which simply serves to rationalize the desires and prejudices of the radical intellectual. In the Middle Ages, however, the lust for knowledge (*libido sciendi*) was considered equally as dangerous to the Christian as the lust for money or the lusts of the flesh, and post-Hiroshima man can scarcely believe so sanguinely in the inevitable goodness of science and human knowledge. These have led not only to destruction but also to manipulativeness, to decreased ability to wonder, sterile objectivity, an evident withering of feeling among many people. Edmund Wilson writes that "The cult of 'reason,' so widely applied in the course of the last three centuries, has come to seem to me in a sense a blind alley." [15] (Anselm Atkins' neat distinction between "money and repressive power" on the one hand and "scientific and intellectual discoveries" on the other is reflective of the peculiar manichean puritanism of some of the radicals, who would prefer to believe that money and power are always oppressive, in the way many Victorians preferred to believe that sex was always lust. In each case the puritan is relieved from having to say anything meaningful on a subject he finds distasteful. The "worldliness" of many radicals often does not extend to their grappling with such perplexing questions as exactly what the proper role of money and power are in society.)

If men's beliefs and attitudes are most readily determined by their peer groups, by those from whom they desire support and approval, then it is largely misleading to measure the beliefs of intellectual Catholics against the beliefs of the secular "silent majority." Measured against the beliefs of his secular counterparts— other progressive intellectuals—the values of the radical Catholic seem to differ very little. Not only do few radical Catholics appear to have any kind of critical perspective on currently fashionable forms of secular radicalism, but there seems virtually no way they could gain such a perspective, at least from their theological principles. By assuming that God's actions and God's will are discovered exclusively in history, and that a better future is coming into existence whose roots are found in present-day progressive movements, they virtually divinize secular radicalism. It is precisely this kind of secular political faith, here disguised with a certain amount of theological language, that has so often perverted idealistic movements into dictatorial police states. Radical Catholics do not desire such an outcome, but their political leap of faith tends to promote it. (Few radical Catholics have seen fit to speak out against the dictatorial, manipulative, intentionally degrading tactics used by some student and black-militant groups, for example.) Radicals do not commonly realize that they have embraced what is in effect a new religion—the faith of radical political action, and that their new god is a jealous god who tolerates no competitors, who demands that the traditional churches be transformed to his worship and that traditional believers either convert or suffer damnation.

In almost every respect the worldly wisdom of the radical Catholic is now merely leftist conventional wisdom. The radical strangeness of the Catholic Worker movement over several decades, the fact (disconcerting both to conservative Catholics and radical non-believers) that orthodox religious belief obviously lies at the heart of Dorothy Day's dissent, is now largely absent from progressive religious circles, and is usually deliberately excluded. There is almost nothing to distinguish the worldly stance of a self-proclaimed "Catholic" radical from that of an atheist or a Jew. Generally dividing the world into enlightened and unenlightened, progressive and static, the radical Catholic does not seem even to admit the possibility of serious dissent from the "enlightened" segment of humanity. Since there is often very little which is Catholic about it (there are exceptions, such as the Berrigan brothers), the term "Catholic Left" seems a misnomer, often a form of parasitic trading on the Church's name. The worldly opinions of many Catholic radicals would be scarcely noticeable or distinctive in progressive circles were it not for the "Catholic" label. Except for the ritualized destruction of draft files, Catholic leftists appear to have contributed little that is unique, original, or distinctive to American dissent. Their ideas attract attention mainly because it is still mildly surprising to secular radicals to find Catholic dissenters at all. The Catholic radical needs the denominational identification, however much he has rejected the substance of the tradition.

The crucial test of the Catholic radical's willingness to confront not just the "straight" secular world but the dissenting world as well is the abortion controversy. Secular progressives seem overwhelmingly to justify abortion, both legally and morally. Many Catholic progressives, who agree with their secular counterparts on all other important issues, who have had little difficulty in utterly repudiating traditional Catholic teaching on birth control, nonetheless hesitate about abortion. Yet on the whole the abortion issue has merely revealed the profound lack of self-confidence which progressive Catholics experience when confronting "the world," their extreme hesitation in criticizing that part of the world which appears to be the enlightened wave of the future. Thus in 1969 *Commonweal* took a moderate editorial stand against abortion, but at the same time felt compelled to add, "It is quite conceivable that in the months to come our opinion on the morality of abortion will change."[16] The journal's editorial stand has not changed formally, but John Deedy has expressed strong annoyance at pressures from Catholic sources against a liberalized New York State abortion law. He quotes an assemblywoman comparing the bishops' tactics to those of the Black Panthers and SDS and finds particularly offensive the fact that a bishop and twelve priests prayed the rosary on the capitol steps in protest against the law. Simultaneously, Mr. Deedy also managed to suggest that the bishops had muted their protests in return for state and to parochial schools [17]—a classic example of an anti-institutionalism which does not scruple over petty consistency. (Nothing in *Commonweal* ordinarily suggests that the editors object to the tactics of SDS and the Black Panthers, and the magazine has favorably reported many confrontations far more disruptive than thirteen priests saying a rosary. While not precisely endorsing abortion-law reform, many progressives would apparently like the Church to allow it to come to pass quietly, with no unseemly protest.)

John G. Milhaven refers to "the current shifting of Christian thinking on abortion" (here "Christian thinking" is again equated with the avant-garde) and says that it illustrates the demise of the ethician, who will give way to "the only pertinent specialist in the matter at hand—the man of scientific and professional experience." [18] Milhaven would almost certainly not concede that the only person qualified to comment on war is the professional soldier, and his formulation mirrors the current conventional wisdom of the American Left—expert testimony must be accepted when it supports "progressive" ideas, but in other areas preeminence must be conceded to the passionate citizen, the moralist without particular technical qualifications. Catholic progressives seem reluctant to believe that on one issue at least—abortion—they may be these passionate citizens, peculiarly fitted through the uniqueness of their tradition to make a valuable dissenting judgment. They are instead apparently prepared to swallow their misgivings and allow history to take its course. Daniel Callahan has written a book, *Abortion: Law, Choice, and Morality* (1970), in which he justifies abortion on demand up to twelve weeks of pregnancy. The editors of the *National Catholic Reporter* have praised Mr. Callahan for his dispassionate and fair evaluation and defend him from the charge of wholly abandoning Catholic teaching.[19] Yet for all his careful distinctions Mr. Callahan advocates a practical legal policy not much different from abortion-on-demand.

The uncertainty in which Catholic progressives now find themselves with respect to abortion is at least in part a result of their failure to turn towards themselves the hard scrutiny they have consistently turned on the hierarchy over the years—the keenness to detect compromise and dishonesty, the questioning of motives, the demands for courageous self-criticism. Sensitive Catholic intellectuals in America have grown up with a deep embarrassment over the backwardness and philistinism of their Church. They have been involved for a long time in loving the progressive, secular intellectual world from afar, usually without requite or at best favored with an occasional patronizing word, nagged by fears of being unworthy of acceptance into this world. Their uncritical enthusiasm for such secular institutions as the university, the public school, liberal social-welfare agencies, has often had this root.

The Catholic attempting to enter this bright world was often counseled in effect to be a "good nigger." In secular universities, for example, the Catholic was expected to be unobtrusive about religion, rarely speaking of it unless others spoke first. If criticism and ridicule were directed at Catholicism, he was to agree with most of it, and if it began to seem misguided and malicious he was to maintain his sense of humor and his restraint. Tolerance, detachment, irony, understatement—these were the civilized virtues uniquely embodied in the "best" schools, and no Catholic could expect to be accepted if he did not practice them. (Abruptly, of course, the radical young secularists began saying that it was precisely these "virtues" which had helped corrupt the university, and they began adopting attitudes and methods not even the most fanatical Catholic decency-crusaders had even thought of employing.)

The ambivalence of the young Catholic intellectual in those conciliar years is exemplified in the shifting attitudes of Michael Novak and Daniel Callahan. In 1962, when Gabriel Marcel spoke at Harvard University, Mr. Novak was ecstatic. When Marcel described his religious conversion ". . . the effect, for some of us . . . in spite of ourselves, and to our own surprise, [was] a joy and a release," and the intellectual histories of the professors seemed insignificant by comparison.[20] The following year Novak called for more active Newman Clubs and stated that ". . . it is not the believer but the unbeliever who is in danger if a living, intellectual faith comes to the campus."[21] By 1965, however, he was admiring the cool, untroubled secularist students for whom religious and metaphysical problems were not significant,[22] just before coolness and unconcern ceased being fashionable on the campuses. At this point Professor Novak, now at Stanford, joined enthusiastically in the new crusading, the new anguish, the new troubled search for identity. In 1967 he reported that radical students showed a hunger for mystical prayer, and the next year he concluded that all Christian values are open to non-Christians and can probably be found better outside the Church than in it.[23]

Also in 1962, a few years before his espousal of secularity, Mr. Callahan was highly impressed by Christopher Dawson's impact on Harvard. The university, he thought, would never be the same. Dawson had shown that God and Christianity are all-pervasive in the West.[24] In 1964 he pointed out that Catholics had difficulty being accepted by secular intellectuals. There were many barriers to be broken down, much concrete history to be overcome.[25] By the following year he had apparently concluded that the barriers were almost all on the believer's side and asked whether Catholics' interest in metaphysics, in ultimate questions, was not itself the primary barrier to their secular involvement.[26]

The radicalism of the young Catholic intellectual of the 1960's was more often than not simply radical uncertainty, a slippery vaccillation between a love of their own tradition and the fear that it was not "relevant" to the world they admired. Usually they resolved the tension in the end by an uncompromising embrace of the world, made possible by a determined rejection of their own tradition and an act of faith that whatever was valuable in that tradition could be found in the world. The unique importance of Catholic intellectuals prior to the late 1960's was precisely their concern for ultimate questions, then distinctly unfashionable among secularists. Long before Norman Mailer discovered existentialism, when it was almost unheard of in the Ivy League, considerable attention was being paid to it in some Catholic universities. By 1970 some young secular radicals were challenging the cool, analytic philosophy of their own universities with observations like, "When a man points a finger at reality, the philosopher studies the finger." American Catholic intellectuals could have provided great resources for the revival of metaphysical concern now manifest among the young, as well as the renewed thirst for spirituality, if they had not been so intimidated by the secular culture. By 1968 Mr. Callahan noted the possibility that Christians were simply mirroring the culture and selling out to it.[27] (Mr. Callahan's writings are sprinkled with potentially devastating criticisms of radical Catholicism, which are mentioned as if to show the author's awareness and then quietly dropped.) Walter Arnold, a lay editor, notes that Eugene Fontinell's philosophy of religion "comes perilously close to [being] a justification of the ways of pragmatism to God and man," and that it virtually forces the denial of most of the special characteristics of religion, including "its sacred and transcendental attributes." However, he also believes it "does not reject anything living of the tradition." [28] Apparently, secular philosophies are now to determine precisely what in the tradition is living and relevant and what not.

Radical Catholics do not appear to reflect very often whether, like conservatives, they are not themselves involved in a kind of unrecognized cultural determinism with respect to the secular worlds they seek to penetrate. Intellectuals are not immune from the same kind of sociological determination which is evident among other classes. Father Robert Drinan, now a Jesuit Congressman, argues, without denying the immorality of the practice, that abortion-on-demand may be preferable to permitting the state to choose which fetuses shall live and which die. (Thus while not admitting that it is morally correct, he gives support to the program of the most extreme abortion-reform advocates.) He opposes the bishops stating dogmatically that abortion is immoral, since they cannot speak for all their people. (As an activist in the peace movement, Father Drinan does not say whether he would find it wrong for a bishop to condemn the Vietnam War against the wishes of many of his people.) He quotes the *Declaration on Religious Liberty of Vatican II* concerning coercion and says it must "surely" apply to Catholics' anti-abortion campaigns.[29] (He does not say why "coercion," that is, legislative lobbying and public propaganda, is wrong for the Church but right for abortion-reform groups or anti-war groups such as some that he is associated with.)

Father Drinan has been quite properly active in liberal circles for some time, circles which include perhaps a minority of Catholics and a substantial number of secularists. At the time that he set forth his ideas on abortion-law reform he was in fact a candidate for Congress, nominated with broad liberal support. It is not surprising that Father Drinan found abortion a vexing issue, one of the few substantial points on which he as a Catholic found himself in disagreement with the secular liberals who made up an important element among his supporters. He admitted that in the course of his campaign he frequently encountered fears about Catholic power left over from the days when birth-control prohibitions were still on the Massachusetts law books.[30] It is not inconceivable that Father Drinan, like so many bishops before him, is willing to sidestep an emotional and divisive moral issue in order to retain the good will of certain people whose respect and support he desires. Just as the late Cardinal Francis Spellman invoked the legitimate ideal of patriotism to silence Catholic opposition to the Vietnam War, so Father Drinan invokes the legitimate principle of religious liberty to silence Catholic protest against abortion. It is not unlikely that as Catholic progressives move more and more into the mainstream of secular liberal society, similar kinds of moral compromises will be justified in a variety of ways. (Catholics who become active in progressive secular circles, for example, sometimes find themselves among people who take marriage rather lightly and approve infidelity. While the Catholics may maintain their own standards, they are often also anxious to eschew the image of being moralistic prudes, and thus they carefully avoid the entire ethical issue. It is true that the Church has grossly overstressed and distorted sexual morality in the past, and that other moral issues are presently more compelling. But it is quite likely that one of the significant contributions Catholics could at present make to their culture would be a sense of sexual restraint, a historically conditioned awareness of the inadequacies of untrammeled sensuality. Catholic radicals, continuously in revolt against their tradition, are not likely to undertake this useful task. Gregory Baum and Antoine Vergote, a Belgian priest-psychologist, are prepared to proclaim that "contemporary eroticism is a revolt against every form of slavery or segregation," [31] conveniently ignoring the many ways in which contemporary eroticism is precisely obsessive, enslaving, and exploitative.)

The articulate radical Catholic of the post-conciliar years has reaped a number of quite tangible rewards—publishing contracts, speaking engagements, invitations to prestigious symposia, attention and approval from Protestant and secular sources, foundation grants, and so on. Although probably very few individuals have been consciously influenced by these considerations, a pervasive sense of belonging in the proper circles has developed—the progressive is pleasantly aware that his own enlightenment has carried him far from his fellow Catholics and brought him close to those who play on the larger stage. He naturally hesitates to jeopardize his place in this world, and a subtle process of self-censorship is often at work whereby the radical senses exactly what is currently acceptable there. A kind of Catholic Uncle-Tomism has developed, in which the "Catholic view" is represented in secular and ecumenical journals, important symposia, university religion departments, by individuals who are seriously

168

estranged from their fellow Catholics, have adopted the major values of the hospitable secular culture, and are sometimes flatteringly anxious to approve that culture.

The struggle on the part of progressives to become relevant to the world generally fails for several reasons, one of them the fact that progressives often do not seem to understand the world as it really is, nor want to. As intellectuals who are oriented towards the secular-intellectual segment of "the world" they prefer to approach reality in terms of intellectual fashions, idealized concepts which often have only a tenuous relationship to what exists on a day-to-day basis. Catholic enthusiasts of secular-city theology, for example, do not seem to realize that Cardinal Spellman was perhaps the most accomplished Catholic secularist America has ever seen. While never losing sight of religious goals as he understood them, he mastered the intricacies of the world's mechanism. He understood how to deal successfully with financiers, politicians, policemen, and generals, all the while retaining the respect of large numbers of ordinary people, despite his unenlightened labor policies. It is only by ignoring perhaps 90 per cent of what exists that Catholic secularizers can talk as they do of "the world."

In a living-room discussion about peace, a young layman of pacific inclinations raises a moral problem very troubling to him. Although he dislikes violence and will not even hunt animals, his wife is a nurse who often works nights in a city hospital. Should he buy her a weapon to keep in her purse? A seminarian present reads a poem by Joan Baez on the beauty of non-violence. The young husband repeats his question, and the seminarian says that as far as he is concerned Joan Baez has said everything necessary on the subject.

This kind of moralizing scarcely differs from the old casuistry, is scarcely less authoritarian, rigid, bookish, or olympian. The "world" to which radical Christians wish to relate is not the world of most men's daily experience. (Black militants now insist that these same white Christians do not relate to them authentically either.) It is often a world of abstractions kept in existence largely in the writings and conversations of intellectuals. Thus when a Protestant theologian, Frederick Herzog, observes that American society is becoming "oppressive" and "totalitarian," he does not feel compelled to work through the difficult and rather ambiguous historical evidence for these assertions but instead "proves" them by footnoting two fashionable pundits—Herbert Marcuse and Erich Fromm (one expert for each adjective).[32] The heralded advent of "political theology" seems to have little relevance to politics as it is ordinarily understood or practiced; it rather deals with romantic concepts of guerilla revolt which are hardly likely to have significant impact in Europe or North America. (Radical Christians often also confuse politics with religion—politics itself becomes the struggle for salvation and moral regeneration.) Christian secularizers fell in love with the abstract idea of cool, anonymous, modern urban living as described by Harvey Cox but at the same time went rushing to create warm, intimate liturgical communities for themselves in the underground Church. These same Christians have now fallen in love with the idealized notion of infinite man, capable of repudiating his past and successfully creating a new world according to his own values and plan. Simultaneously, however, their actual experience of the world, which they share with many secularists, is pessimistic and bitter. The realistic possibilities for significant progress seem slight in comparison with the massive weight of established society. Those who begin with a blind trust in their own powers always end the most buffeted by fate and history. Present-day Christian radicals seem to lack a sense of the massive givens of existence, which must be wrestled with in their own terms. Too often tentative, sketchy ideas have hardened quickly into programs to remake the world.

A former nun, a member of the underground Church, boasts that she is "living on the sense level" (the smell of fresh-baked bread, and so on),[33] as though the ability to sense were a new discovery of her particular coterie and as though there have not been very many cardinals and stockbrokers, even Gestapo agents, with keen palates and sharp noses. (In fact, many radical Catholics discredit their own wordliness by purporting to find cheap drugstore wine delicious.) A middle-aged Sacred Heart nun, who has spent most of her life amid the traditional pieties and conservative educational practices of her order, is now able to endorse with absolute assurance the fashionable modern theories—the need for "relevance," "space-oriented" vs. "time-oriented" classes, the school as a supermarket (students will choose challenging courses as a housewife chooses anchovies), the knowledge explosion, and the inevitable good results of the new methods (former high-school dropouts will within two years learn to use language properly, think critically, understand mathematics, and appreciate their own place in cultural history).[34] In numerous ways Catholic progressives demonstrate that as old certitudes are discredited, new ones will be seized upon with eagerness, in the form of abstract stereotypes about the world.

The progressives' taste for abstractions and for simplistic formulas is very much a part of their understanding of themselves and their Church as well. Thus Anselm Atkins gives the following summary of nineteenth-century religious history: "In America

. . . the churches substituted the newfangled capitalist-imperialist policies for their own original message, while keeping the old religious symbols as if nothing had changed. . . . The Church became the guardian of the Status Quo." [35] This is vulgar Marxism sufficient to make a serious left-wing historian blush, but it is useful to radicals because it justifies their jettisoning of a past which has become burdensome to them. Hidden in the "humanism" of most Christian radicals is a view of history which consigns to perdition the majority of human beings who have ever lived, or who now live, and finds virtue and meaning only in the saving few of each generation. When secularized Christians talk about what is "human" they are drawn irresistibly to the dramatic—drug addiction, extreme poverty, courageous moral witness, artistic creation, deep personal agony. The quest for minimum economic security, the raising of children, recreation—the ordinary things which make up the bulk of most people's lives—are generally ignored in this new humanism. When Andrew Greeley proclaimed the need for Christians to be filled with joy, a Virginia housewife mentioned these inconspicuous mundane truths and St. Teresa's prayer to know reality, which she hoped would be granted "especially to those who assume the job of mass communication." [36]

Whatever chance Catholics now have of making themselves and their religion relevant to the world surely does not lie in the direction so many radicals have pointed to—the virtual abandonment of everything distinctive in their tradition and a total willingness to embrace the customs and beliefs of the "enlightened" segment of the modern world. If the influence of Catholicism in this world is minimal, this is at least in part because secularists

172

are now aware that many of the Catholics they encounter, who represent Catholicism to the sophisticated public, have little internalized religion and few private beliefs, take scant nourishment from anything in their tradition. Brother Gabriel Moran points out that ". . . as religion is made more 'relevant' in school curriculums it eventually seems to be absorbed into everything else." (He thinks this may be a good thing.)[37] In miniature this is the problem of Christian secularism—if nothing of importance really sets off the Christian from the world then there is little point in even using the term "Christian" or attempting to keep the Christian churches alive by making them more and more secular. A Jewish theologian, Eugene Borowitz, says, "Contemporary Christianity may be agog with secularity. Since we were in it up to our nostrils for several decades, we know we are men of faith precisely because we must move beyond it. We obviously do not believe as much as our grandfathers did, but we have discovered painfully that we believe far more than our society." [38]

But Gregory Baum urges a new theology in which God is found entirely in the world and in human events, and that "we need not add him to it [the world] by our pious thoughts." Man's worldly pursuits—friendship, work, literature, social involvement —are the places where redemption touches men's lives. The task of the Church, according to Father Baum, is merely to intensify this redemptive mystery.[39] The problem with this now common formula is that for many Catholics it has proved even less meaningful than the old piety. Large numbers of progressive Catholics who, after the Council, began to see secular involvement as the true meaning of their faith discovered soon that secular involvement was enough. The Church could not deepen this for them in any important way. The problem that so many progressives have experienced—lack of meaning in their religion —is really a self-created problem which is insoluble so long as the terms remain unchanged. Religion must involve some reality distinct from and superior to human life on earth, or there is no possible way it can be made meaningful. Many Christians are experiencing failure of nerve, the inability any longer to affirm radically strange and (in Kierkegaard's sense) absurd beliefs in the teeth of modern scepticism. Secularists can scarcely respect such persons or assume that Christianity has anything of significance worth their attention. Like compulsive efforts to win love, compulsive efforts to be "relevant" usually have the reverse effect.

To be truly relevant at this point Catholics must begin facing the question that Borowitz poses—what does the believer believe which is somehow "more" than his culture? Catholicism need not be antagonistic to liberal secularism, although there will inevitably be times (as on the abortion question) when it will have to be. But at the least it must endeavor to be complementary to that culture and not content itself with the truly irrelevant, and dishonest, role of endorsing in religious language every development in the world which appears to promise a better future. If Catholicism has nothing to tell the world which the world does not already know, then it should simply pass out of existence. The best service that believers could now do the world would be a bold and joyful proclamation of the Good News in quite specific terms—the reality of God, Christ's redemption, God's personal and continuing love for all men, victory over death in Christ. (Among conspicuous Catholic radi-

174

cals only Father Daniel Berrigan seems to be forging a stance quite obviously and openly nourished by his religious tradition, and only he acknowledges acting out of a religious sense which many other radicals would probably regard as naive and obsolete. In contrast to Father Berrigan, who embraces celibacy, sees himself becoming a true contemplative, and reads Scripture and St. John of the Cross to sustain himself, is the radical Carmelite Nicholas Riddell, also a draft-file burner. According to another sympathetic Carmelite, Father Riddell once was nourished by John of the Cross and Teresa of Avila but now talks only of Eldridge Cleaver, Franz Fanon, and Rap Brown. He regards meditation and asceticism as irrelevant. His fellow Carmelite, although editor of a journal devoted to the spiritual life, apparently sees no need to explain what the Church or the priesthood could possibly mean to Father Riddell besides useful names to attach to himself.[40]) In a time of almost universal political despair Christians are uniquely able to offer the world a joyful hope—that when man is weary, and his best efforts have failed, God may still intervene.

There is a great deal of courage in the Church's conservative stand of defining itself with precision, making its beliefs explicit, and inviting an either-or response, which in recent times has perhaps been increasingly negative. Radicals should recognize this as an existential posture, insofar as an institution is capable of such. By defining itself the Church exposes its vulnerabilities and invites rejection; when rejected it does not surrender its unique identity but continues to affirm it. In doing so it may exasperate many people who wish it to be something it is not, to conform itself to prevailing cultural mores.

175

Anselm Atkins predicts that "the serious theology of the next thirty years will be on the way to becoming anthropology . . . and politics," but theologians must still master the core tradition of theology to keep from being swallowed up by these other disciplines. Dogma will become primarily the history of dogma, little more.[41] This prescription for the theologian is the dilemma of the radical Christian generally—if the tradition is simply treated as history, how can it prevent anyone from being swallowed up, from losing even the barest perceptible Christian identity?

At the end of the Council, Daniel Callahan made a penetrating critique of what would soon be the spirit of the new ecumenism. He saw two possibilities for the progressive Catholic—to accept the Catholic tradition as primary, although broadening it with other insights, or to relegate it to the status of merely one tradition among many. The latter option, he warned, would be just as devastating as formal schism.[42] He had not foreseen a third possibility, which some radicals have pursued—the virtual rejection of the Catholic tradition altogether and an openness to meaning everywhere but in the Church. Replying to Michael Novak's description of Christianity as "a point of view, a horizon," he said this was "neither rich nor strong enough to take account of Christ's absolute demands and self-revelation, and discriminating enough to distinguish Christianity from a philosophical or ideological world view."[43] The following year he wrote,

The word "church" would mean absolutely nothing unless it was possible to say what the bounds and norms are. It is no less nonsensical to hold that every person should be free to set up his own standards for membership. . . . If the community claims to share a

176

common faith—and it would have to in order to call itself a religious community—then the community must have the courage and the rationality to say what this faith is, and in some detail.[44]

Part of the progressives' failure to make their religion relevant to the world stems from their failure to appreciate the worldly wisdom already present in their tradition. As modern liturgists point out, the Catholic belief about life after death logically requires the kind of funeral liturgy which has now replaced the old *Requiem*—an emphasis on hope, joy, and resurrection. But the beauty and power of the *Requiem* lay precisely in its compromise with the world, its accommodation of the feelings of sorrow, fear, and despair which in reality most believers probably experience at the death of those they love, along with the promise of deliverance. The unreformed Church was never so removed from men's needs as modern reformers believe. For a long time, progressives thought that modern man had progressed beyond his fear of death, that cool, practical Westerners had no need of the psychic crutch of belief in the hereafter. By now it is obvious that Americans merely suppress thoughts of death, and pretend not to be interested, just as the Victorians feigned lack of interest in sex. The need to "solve" the problem of death is once more becoming respectable. Father Baum, however, insists that the Christian message does not proclaim eternal life (radicals do not feel bound to the clear meaning of the Scripture when it seems to them unenlightened) but rather that man should not fear death and should accept it gracefully.[45] Thus radicals, by their infidelity to their own tradition, seem once more about to lose the opportunity of making a uniquely important contribution to their culture.

Notes

1. *The Critic,* June-July, 1968, p. 13.
2. Colaianni, *The Catholic Left,* p. 21.
3. *Journal of Ecumenical Studies,* Spring, 1969, p. 228.
4. *The New Yorker,* Oct. 26, 1970, p. 114.
5. *Commonweal,* Oct. 7, 1966, p. 5.
6. *Ibid.,* Sept. 6, 1968, p. 601, and July 24, 1970, p. 375; *National Catholic Reporter,* July 10, 1970, p. 12.
7. *Commonweal,* April 4, 1969, p. 66.
8. Carling, *Move Over!,* p. 127.
9. DuBay, *The Human Church,* p. 63.
10. *Commonweal,* Dec. 29, 1967, p. 405.
11. *National Catholic Reporter,* May 22, 1970, p. 7; May 15, 1970, p. 7.
12. *The New Yorker,* Oct. 25, 1969, p. 160. (All quotes from *The New Yorker.*)
13. *St. Louis Review,* July 10, 1970, p. 4.
14. *Commonweal,* Feb., 13, 1970, p. 539.
15. Quoted by Malcolm Muggeridge, *Esquire,* Oct., 1969, p. 44.
16. *Commonweal,* March 17, 1969, p. 668.
17. *Ibid.,* May 1, 1970, p. 154.
18. *Ibid.,* Oct. 31, 1969, p. 140.
19. *National Catholic Reporter,* Aug. 7, 1970, p. 15.
20. *Commonweal,* Oct. 5, 1962, p. 31.
21. *Ibid.,* Jan. 5, 1963, p. 452.
22. *Generation of the Third Eye,* pp. 164-5.
23. *Commonweal,* April 28, 1967, pp. 174-5; Nov. 1, 1968, p. 158.
24. *Ibid.,* June 15, 1962, p. 294.
25. *Ibid.,* Nov. 20, 1964, p. 271.
26. *Ibid.,* Nov. 12, 1965, p. 189.
27. *The Critic,* June-July, 1968, p. 13.
28. *Commonweal,* Sept. 25, 1970, p. 486.
29. *Ibid.,* April 17, 1970, pp. 108-9.
30. *Ibid.,* June 12, 1970, p. 303.
31. *National Catholic Reporter,* Sept. 25, 1970, p. 6.
32. *Continuum,* Winter, 1970, p. 521.

33. Quoted by Michael Novak, *Saturday Evening Post*, Dec. 28, 1968, p. 66.

34. *St. Louis Post-Dispatch*, April 29, 1970, p. 4F.

35. *Commonweal*, Feb. 13, 1970, p. 538.

36. *National Catholic Reporter*, June 5, 1970, p. 7.

37. *Continuum*, Autumn, 1969, p. 414.

38. *Commentary*, Nov., 1969, p. 90.

39. *St. Louis Review*, Oct. 10, 1969, p. 12.

40. For Father Berrigan see *The New Yorker*, July 25, 1970, pp. 20-23. For Father Riddell see the article by Peter Thomas Rohrbach, O.C.D., *The Catholic World*, June, 1970, pp. 116-9.

41. *Commonweal*, Oct. 31, 1969, pp. 150, 152.

42. *Ibid.*, Sept. 24, 1965, p. 696.

43. *Ibid.*, Nov. 12, 1965, p. 189.

44. *Ibid.*, April 1, 1966, p. 54.

45. *St. Louis Review*, May 8, 1970, p. 12.

7.

The Crisis of the Spirit

THE bitterest failure of the years of reform in the Church has been the evident failure of spiritual regeneration, which seems to have been Pope John's principal hope for the Council. Few people claim to feel closer to God as a result of the reforms of the past decade, whatever other good effects the reforms have had. There is an obvious spiritual malaise affecting both religious and laymen.

One of the ways in which post-conciliar radicals fail to be radical is in their implicit agreement with the hierarchy that it is the structure of the Church which primarily matters—the hierarchy tends to equate Catholicism with the well being of the structure, the radicals tend to blame the structure for all the Church's ills. Ordinarily, the formation of such groups as the National Association of Laymen or the National Priests' Association might be a healthy thing. At present, however, it reflects the prevalence of an unrecognized heresy—salvation through politics.

As progressives never cease pointing out, traditional Catholicism often implied a rote kind of religion—blind submission to a collection of rules and prescribed practices, external conformity as an adequate substitute for inner fervor, and indeed in some cases preferable to it. The vision of certain pre-conciliar reformers was the interiorization of belief, the kindling of personal fires in many souls, and this was the logical antidote to the formalism of the unreformed Church. But many reformers found that, having been raised in a formalistic milieu which was indifferent to interiority, they were not capable either of developing it in themselves or communicating it to others. Their notion of reform inexorably became a new version of externality —salvation through action in the world or salvation through reform of Church structures.

The "crisis of authority" which has so dominated both conservative and progressive thought since the Council is a real crisis. But it is also a cover which is used, half-consciously, to obscure the deeper spiritual crisis exposed by the collapse of so many traditions and so many structures. The almost desperate concentration of certain radical Catholics on "democratizing" the Church, with discrediting traditional laws, beliefs, and authorities, often seems a way of avoiding the gnawing inner emptiness, the deep religious confusion, which must somehow be overcome if *aggiornamento* is to have any reality. Monica Baldwin, an Englishwoman who left the convent thirty years ago and wrote *I Leap Over the Wall,* now repents her action and attributes it, among other things, to her neglect of prayer. She points out that in the writings of Charles Davis there is much talk about structural faults in the Church and oppressive authorities, but little about prayer and the interior life.[1] The same observation could be made about most radical spokesmen of the post-conciliar years—they can focus with force, originality, and precision on everything about the Church except its core meaning, which is man's encounter with God in the depths of his spirit. The rejection of the sacred is an integral part of the process which the French Protestant theologian Jacques Ellul sees as the tyranny of technique—ends are systematically and ruthlessly transformed into means only. A commonplace radical question about sacred doctrines and practices is, "What good are they?"

As Michael Novak once observed, in pragmatic, secular America it is almost impossible for religious faith to take intelligent root.[2] The decline of religious belief in the modern world seems roughly correlative with prosperity and economic and technological advancement. (This is also roughly the view of the matter given by the prophets in the Old Testament.) It is not therefore surprising, nor necessarily reprehensible, that many sincere Christians should experience great difficulty in maintaining a lively faith in God, that their religious faith seems to weaken progressively amid the pressures of their culture. What is surprising, and is reprehensible, is that so many Christians should not only accede to this weakening of faith, but embrace it and even seek to discredit the faith which some of their co-religionists have been able to sustain.

Thus Mary Daly says that faith is merely a "deeper questioning" and it is therefore impossible to lose one's faith.[3] (This formula is one means by which radicals seek to place themselves beyond criticism. Since personal searching alone matters, the individual is always "right," no matter what position he embraces.) Father Eugene Schallert says that "The man who says he has found God is a fool," [4] thus effectively condemning Jewish patriarchs, Catholic saints, and the great heroes of historic Protestantism, as well as countless numbers of ordinary believers throughout history. William DuBay says that "Knowledge of God is not only impossible but inhuman," and that "The only trouble with Christian education today is that it attempts to teach people about God." He virtually equates religion with

182

ethics.[5] Father James T. Burtchaell, a Notre Dame theologian, insists that God can be known only in dealings with other men. "There are no direct transactions with the Father; no one has ever spoken to him, no one has ever heard him. . . ," [6] he insists, thus dogmatically and arrogantly invalidating the countless varieties of religious experience found among people of all centuries and all religious persuasions.

In a celebrated trumpet-call to secularity, "Religious Slum-Dwellers," Daniel Callahan in 1966 confessed that there was nothing in his experience which he was tempted to call transcendent and reported the experience of many contemporary Catholics who had come to find work in the world far more satisfying than anything having to do with religion. He concluded, "There are many mansions in the kingdom of God and there is one, perhaps, for those whose spirit never soars but only muddles along in the empirical, the finite, the limited." [7] What was here formulated by Mr. Callahan in modest terms quickly hardened into dogma, however, in which the Catholic secularist has often seemed to resent the beliefs of those who profess some soaring of the spirit. Rosemary Ruether speaks of the necessary total destruction of the sacred.[8] Terry Eagleton says that the inherent meaning of Christianity is political, with no distinct "spiritual life." [9] Mr. Callahan himself by 1969 was beginning to react rather peevishly even to modest expressions of religious faith. He took Father Gregory Baum to task for speaking of a contemporary experience of the Gospel and asked how Father Baum could know any religious truths, implying that if they were honest (that is, at 3 A.M., after a few drinks), progressives would admit that the new theology was as meaningless to them as the old.[10] (The notion that men are necessarily more honest at 3 A.M. after a few drinks is a typical piece of liberal-Catholic pseudo-worldliness.)

Kathy McHale Mulherin, a young Catholic New Leftist, has candidly confessed the psychology behind much of this new anti-religiousness: "The Council also defined the relationship between man and God as horizontal, if you will: man made contact with God through other men. . . . Inasmuch as I had suffered agonies all those years in school because I couldn't *find* God, never knew whether God knew about *me,* I was immensely relieved to come upon this discovery. I was also angry, for the energy I had poured into the search for God now seemed a waste of time." [11] Martin Luther, similarly beset by his inability to experience God's personal love for him, struggled through to his most profound religious awareness. The modern radical, however, concludes from his own dryness of soul that awareness of God is unimportant, if real, and is probably illusory. A layman argues that, since Paul Tillich, Christians have no solid grounds for thinking that a personal, loving God exists and prayer is therefore called into question. With Rudolf Bultmann (again the authorities are summoned) "the wise man" reinterprets religious beliefs "guided by current philosophy." The Church will continue in difficulty until it too embraces this new theology. [12] Sometimes radicals are embarrassed by strongly religious individuals. Carolyn R. Shaffer, a theology student, patronizingly suggested, after Martin Buber's death, that he was really a secularist without knowing it, teaching a secular message with mere religious trappings. "God-talk" was not really relevant to his thought, she argued, merely an appendage. [13] (This is the kind of intellectual imperialism which once led medieval theologians to claim pagan sages as secret

Christians. It is the mentality which cannot endure the thought of wisdom existing in an uncongenial milieu.)

What was formerly called the faith problem—the credibility of belief, the ability to sustain a living sense of God—is perhaps the single most crucial problem afflicting the contemporary Church. Many individuals of deep intelligence, virtue, and good will now find themselves beset by the greatest uncertainties, the barest glimmer of what they once serenly called their faith. As Mr. Callahan once requested, a mansion must be reserved for such people in the house of the Church. Further, they must be respected and the fact must be acknowledged that their doubts have certain cleansing and medicinal effects on the faith, and that as modern men no Catholics can be wholly immune from these same uncertainties. What cannot be allowed, however, is for these individuals to be accorded positions of dominance, that they be allowed to decide the Church's character and programs for the coming generation, and that they invalidate, subtly undermine, and suppress the frank religious faith which the majority of Catholics probably still maintain. It is precisely this dominance, however, that the confessedly uncertain radicals now seems to desire.

Radicals who are so adept at discovering corruptions in the Church wrought by capitalism and the American spirit should be sensitive also to the subversion of religious reform by a quintessential American heresy—pragmatic activism. Since the Council, many progressives have abandoned, tacitly or otherwise, the hard struggles with faith, with prayer, with interiority, and spirit which are so vexing to everyone, and have plunged into "the world" and its struggles with a massive act of faith that here, somehow, meaning and truth, even God, are to be found.

As with the old passive piety, there are degrees of depth and sophistication here. But for many the new commitment to signing petitions, walking in picket lines, tutoring in ghettoes, is the same kind of rote, external, salvation-through-action as mechanically thumbing rosaries used to be. Among other things it is a way of avoiding the confrontation with the self, and with God.

Sheila Moriarty insists that life itself reveals God and that no specific "religious" interests are necessary.[14] The Dominican theologian Thomas F. O'Meara is sure that God will be found in "conscientious service of society," contemporary art, "the positive and pragmatic view of the fture," and protests against military power, racism, urban exploitation. The "movement" (roughly in the New Left sense) is doing God's work. "The explosions of knowledge and technical control . . . [are] signs of the Spirit working with man."[15] (With the Catholic liberal's usual lack of worldly knowledge, Father O'Meara seems unaware that many members of the "movement" abominate all forms of the knowledge explosion and technical control.) A parish priest in New York State urges the Church to stop wasting time and energy in theological debate and self-preservation and begin the task of feeding the hungry. To this he adds, as the next crucial task, his own pet secular cause—reducing the hours which children must go to school and revamping the state educational bureaucracies.[16]

The basic point which these secularizers wish to make—that God can be encountered in the world and that religion cannot have meaning only in the sanctuary—is, of course, a valid one, and a necessary corrective to certain older ascetic theories. But this secular Christianity has now become imperialistic and ex-

THE CRISIS OF THE SPIRIT

clusivist. It seeks to deny, with deep arrogance and presumption, the specifically "religious" experiences of many believers throughout history. Instead of proposing alternative paths to God, most radicals apparently wish to close off all possibility of what was formerly called the spiritual life. They proclaim dogmatically that their own failure to undergo religious experiences, in the traditional sense, is necessarily normative for the whole Church, and that those who claim these experiences are deluded. Often they attempt to discredit traditional piety by positing a necessary connection between it and moral blindness. Thus Michael Novak says, about the Mass, "a man who offers bread to God when other men starve for lack of bread has not yet understood the Gospel of Jesus Christ." [17] (Radicals often urge that money spent on religion should be used for the poor. Rarely do they suggest this same use for money spent on books and records, liquor and marijuana, sensitivity training and travel.) It is of course true that many persons of deep piety have been indifferent to glaring moral evils, that the old piety often turned people inward in such a way as to make them oblivious to their neighbors. But the solution to this failing was for reformers precisely to knit together the two strands—of religion as traditionally understood, and action in the world. Instead, most seem to have opted for the dissolution of one side of the tension, in the blind hope that nothing of value will be thereby lost.

But there has probably been no more serious miscalculation in the whole of *aggiornamento* than the radicals' assumption that "religion" was dead. As early as 1967, while secularization theology was at its height, Paul Goodman was already observing that the questions being asked by radical young people were really religious questions, and it was primarily the campus chaplains'

187

own lack of faith which prevented them from seeing this fact.[18] By the end of the decade this had become a commonplace, and many students proudly described themselves as religious and expressed a credulity about things supernatural which far exceeded the beliefs of most Church members. Catholic radicals were predictably unprepared for this twist of history, and had to scramble desperately to relate to it. Some radical clerics who had defined for themselves a role based exclusively on political activism now found themselves once again being asked about prayer and about God. Presumably, these were questions which they as clergy were uniquely fitted to answer, but often this proved not to be the case. One of the greatest scandals of the post-conciliar Church has been precisely this unpreparedness, this wanton neglect of their own special vocations, by so many clergy and Christian laity. The pathetic self-doubt and spiritual emptiness of so many Catholics was revealed in the fact that, having effectively abandoned religion as meaningless, they hastened to reclaim it merely because certain people in "the world" now told them it was valid. The utter incompetence of such Catholics to act as religious leaders in any sense was revealed both to the Church and to the world. (In 1970 there was a brief flurry of controversy over whether the Beatles' song "Let It Be" embodied references to the Blessed Virgin. Some progressives who had rejected Marian devotions long before were apparently ready to resume them if only the Beatles' endorsement could be proven.[19])

In scrambling to relate themselves to this unexpected religious revival, Catholic radicals have probably again tied themselves to a passing bit of historical ephemera. It is dubious that any profound religious regeneration will emerge from the present fashionable preoccupation with psychedelic drugs, rituals, and mystical experiences. Certain aspects of this new religiosity reveal how the decline of the Church's credibility is due in part merely to fashions among the avant-garde rather than to anything specific to the Church's creed. If a few years ago young radicals rejected the Church because it taught irrelevant, archaic, and incredible doctrines, they are now prepared (temporarily) to accept the most bizarre teachings of astrology and pop mysticism. For persons who discount the Resurrection of the Lord but guide their lives according to the changes of the *I Ching,* only one term seems appropriate—bad faith. Radical Catholics who hope to find in the present religiosity a path to the religion of the future are likely to be disappointed. When sophisticated people suddenly become credulous over magic and amateur mysticism it is almost always a sign of the total breakdown of the religious and moral values which had formerly guided their lives. The new religiosity is then either a desperate lunging towards new certainties or a perverse wallowing in the breakdown of the old.

The rediscovery of the centrality of religion is also having the effect, among some Catholic progressives, of permitting the burial of the Church with a different eulogy than the one previously pronounced over it. First the radicals laid Catholicism to rest because they discovered that "religion" was a pernicious illusion. Now they can rebury it with the assurance that, while religion is crucial to human life, it exists better without the Church. Thus Michael Novak is astonished at how few Christians pray, while radical students show a hunger for mystical prayer. Prayer, however, is for Novak a form of intensified self-knowledge, so that even atheists pray frequently.[20] Donald Cutler says that ". . . the

189

entire society is teeming with religious elements—myths, ideas, roles, groups." [21] Sister Seraphim Karper, a cloistered nun, believes that "modern man . . . will soon find the realm of contemplative, religious experience co-natural," and that modern artists, having finally triumphed over the dark places of the human soul, have once more mastered the inner dynamisms, so that a new age of religious creativity is about to dawn.[22] Unintentionally perhaps, such understandings of religion doom religion as it has been historically understood, precisely by absorbing it into everything else. It is the final and most subtle temptation to which radicals seem in the process of succumbing.

Genuine secularists rarely seem as willing as radical Christians to equate religious and secular values. Thus Edmund Wilson, who has always been a thorough secularist, says:

I am aware that, for those of real religious vocation, their religious transcendences and revelations are as real as anything else in their lives, that they may be, in fact, more real than anything else. . . . This vision of God's light I have never had, no moment of exaltation has ever made me feel that I was close to God, but I know that this has been felt by a variety of other human beings in a variety of situations and in a variety of earthly environments . . .[23]

This is perhaps the best possible starting place for any understanding of religion in a sceptical age—the personal sense of God's reality and God's actions which some people seem to possess and others do not. The validity of these subjective beliefs cannot, of course, be proven in any satisfactory way, nor can those who possess them be considered superior human beings to those who do not. But such beliefs do constitute, at the very least, a uniquely valuable part of the human heritage, and it is the principal task of organized religion in this age to preserve, encourage, and develop these beliefs. Certainly, there is no other organ of society which will do so.

The intention of many Christian radicals, however, seems to be precisely the opposite. Mary Daly questions how Catholics can know that Christ was the definitive revelation of God and free from sin. If this is faith, she insists, then it is merely what Paul Tillich calls "the will to believe" and is the source of psychic illnesses.[24] Modern theologians refuse to tell man what he must believe, but they are quite eager to tell him what he must not believe. Strangely, this new scepticism is often brought forward under the aegis of "humility" and is contrasted to the "arrogance" of traditional Christians, although genuine humility would seem to require a willingness to admit at least the possibility that others might possess religious sensitivities lacking to oneself. The "religious slum-dweller," in Mr. Callahan's phrase, now shows himself highly imperialistic. He is no longer content with a room in the mansion but wants the entire house, and is quite prepared to burn the house down if he does not receive title. The etiquette of religious progressivism forbids criticizing non-believers in any substantial way, but it positively encourages treating believers as deluded, childish, neurotic fools.

The radicals' central concern with "institutions" does them good service here, since properly religious concerns can be readily dismissed as mere "institutional hangups." The New York priest who is so eager to enlist the Church in the fight to reform elementary education insists that "the Christian Church must stop wasting time, energy, and money in theological debate and self-preservation . . ."[25] Yet the abandonment of "theological debate" implies either that theological certainty has been rediscovered (a judgment which no radical would of course accept) or else that

191

it is unimportant to think about one's beliefs. (There is a third possibility which too often seems to be correct—that one has no religious beliefs worth thinking about.)

In the minds of many conservative Catholics the movement for reform in the Church is an attempt to substitute politics for religion, forcibly to remold the Church into a vehicle for radical social change. This view is obviously highly oversimplified, but it is nonetheless an opinion which receives strong support in the writings of certain radicals such as Terry Eagleton and Rosemary Ruether, for whom "religion" is a dirty word unless it can somehow be directly related to radical politics.

Beyond the explicit statement of this position by a few radicals, it is not unreasonable to suspect that political concern has been the dominating, if only half-recognized, motivation of many other radical and reformist leaders since the Council. There is a particular view of the Catholic masses which has gained general acceptance in progressive circles and which is somewhat as follows: "(1) The laity are basically reactionary, and obstacles to social justice. (2) The source of their reaction is their excessive preoccupation with 'churchy' matters—dogmas, devotions, moral rules—which keep them from a larger sympathy with 'the world.' (3) If these 'churchy' things are eliminated or drastically downgraded the laity may become more open to the true meaning of the Gospel, which implies social involvement."

The recovery of a strong sense of social concern has been one of the greatest blessings of *aggiornamento,* and radicals and progressives deserve great credit for this achievement. But it has also blinded them in certain ways, as preoccupation with any great idea always has a partially blinding effect. In particular, this recovery of the social dimension of Christianity has spawned certain fallacies which progressives are reluctant to confront. They have, for example, stereotyped the Catholic layman much as white racists stereotype blacks—when a Catholic radical visualizes the average layman he apparently sees a Polish-American on Chicago's Southside throwing rocks at integrationist nuns. Yet a 1970 Louis Harris Poll, commissioned by the National Urban League, finds that Irish-, Polish-, and Italian-Americans are in general much less prejudiced against blacks than are Anglo-Saxon Protestants. Only a minority of these ethnic groups express segregationist sentiments.[26] Even the political benightedness which does infect these groups is only connected with their traditional piety by an assumption—there is no evidence that orthodox piety is the source of political reaction, or that elimination of orthodox piety will induce political enlightenment. (It is not inconceivable that the imputed connection between religious orthodoxy and political reaction is in some cases a self-serving assumption on the part of those who make it. As they feel their own traditional beliefs slipping away they can justify this situation on the ground that it is necessary to their political commitment.)

However worthy the cause, Catholic traditionalists have a legitimate right to be resentful and suspicious if they think they are being manipulated for political ends, and no one can say with certainty what the limits of this political influence are at present, especially since it is not always a conscious factor. But sweeping theological reformulations sometimes seem motivated by an urgent desire to make the Church "relevant" to the world, understood as the political avant-garde, and it is not unreasonable to suspect that certain kinds of radical theologizing—the questioning of Christ's physical Resurrection, for example, or of the Real Presence—has the aim of making Catholicism less "supernatural," hence hopefully more in tune with contemporary social needs. To the extent that this is so, the legitimacy of this kind of theology is largely vitiated by alien factors. It is a process no different from that of formulating a theology for the purpose of legitimizing hierarchical power, or secular monarchy, or colonialism.

Radical Catholics sometimes make an easy equation of piety and politics which does not begin to solve the problem. Father Gerard Sloyan says that "any group or movement that continues to heed the cry of the poor will continue to lead in good prayer." [27] This is an appealing formulation but unfortunately one which seems to lack empirical evidence. There are innumerable secular groups which heed the cry of the poor but seem to have not the slightest interest in prayer. There are now some Christian groups which have discovered that the more they come to the aid of the poor, the less interested they are in liturgy or prayer of any kind. Father John McKenzie says, "it is the one commandment to love your neighbor as yourself, and thus to fulfill the commandment of loving God." [28] Apart from the questionable procedure of merging into one commandment two which Christ explicitly kept distinct, Father McKenzie does not reflect on what value, if any, explicit Christianity can possibly have, since men are obviously capable of loving their neighbors without it.

Although America is officially religious, the actual thrust of American culture is really anti-religious. Not only is religion officially banned from public education, thus inculcating the impression that it is false or unimportant, but of all the options open to man probably none is so lethal towards true religion as pragmatic technocracy. Those places in the world where religion appears to be declining are mainly those places where Western pragmatic technocracy has been strongly influential, and although they often revile this spirit in the abstract, religious radicals in their embrace of secularity really assume the superiority of this pragmatism. When religion becomes incredible in a particular culture they assume there is something sick about religion rather than the culture. Their radicalism is thus very limited. Daniel Callahan once suggested that secularity might allow for man's "supernatural aspirations," adding, "We shall see." [29] But to a religious person this formulation can only seem backwards. There is no obvious justification for granting secularity a normative status, so that religion is permissible only if it can be fitted in with secularity. It is just as possible that secularity, as the modern West experiences it, is really an aberration in the total life of mankind.

Religion in the modern West is usually linked, both by traditionalists and innovators, with morality. Countless young Catholics have drifted out of the Church because, as habitual violators of the Church's rigid sexual code, they could see no reason to keep belonging. Religious teachers who were unable to inculcate in them a real spirituality settled for the much easier achievement of impressing on them a strict personal morality bearing religious sanction. Countless modern Catholics have also drifted out of the Church because, having decided that moral concern was the essence of their faith, they found nothing distinctive about that faith and nothing in the Church they could not find somewhere else. They too were never introduced to a real spirituality transcending ethics.

It is probably more meaningful, however, to assimilate religion to aesthetics rather than to ethics, and the problem of religious meaning and religious identity can be approached much more easily in this way. The modern religious man is then seen not as necessarily morally superior to the non-religious man, so that conspicuous moral failures on the part of Christians are sufficient to discredit the Church, but rather as a man with a peculiar sensitivity—towards God, towards the sacred, towards transcendence—which in most men is badly underdeveloped. This religious sensitivity does not guarantee that the religious man will be morally superior to the non-religious, or more intelligent or more humanly sensitive. Great artists, and great connoisseurs of art have often had nothing to recommend them as people except their special exalted sensitivities. Men of towering compassion and deep moral fervor conversely often lack all aesthetic sense. Both the reality found in beauty and the reality found in religion are at least in part transcendent, and thus they transcend the individual flawed men who catch glimpses of these realities but are not taken up wholly into them. At the deepest level, however, all art is profoundly moral, and so also all religion is profoundly moral. Error consists in attempting to make the connection too easily and mechanically, so that men of obvious moral weakness are assumed to be incapable of appreciating beauty or knowing God, and art or religion which seeks to serve noble moral ends is assumed therefore to be profound and genuine. Much art has been created for good moral purposes which is empty and tawdry, and much of what passes for relevant religion in this age also seems shallow and unnourishing. Man continues to believe that the good, the true, and the beautiful must somehow be ultimately one, but it is a continuing demonstration of the sinful, fragmentary character of our world that this unity is so elusive.

If religion is regarded as akin to the aesthetic sense, although with deep moral roots as well, it is obvious that there are degrees and kinds of religious sensibilities just as there are of artistic sensibilities. Some persons, who may be morally or intellectually quite attractive human beings, may be totally insensitive to aesthetic and/or religious realities. Music, literature, or painting of all kinds may seem trivial and meaningless to them, actually a distraction from the great moral or intellectual problems which obsess them. Other persons, who may have the same high moral and intellectual concerns or who may be quite ordinary people, have an aesthetic sense which is real but limited and rather vulgar—they appreciate only art which is obvious and sentimental. There is a religious equivalent of this in the simple folk pieties which even sophisticated Catholics have often embraced in the past. Persons who combine deep aesthetic appreciation, religious awareness, intellectual profundity, and moral concern are quite rare. Society needs all these, and while pre-eminent importance should perhaps be given to the moral man, it would be disastrous for society if moral concern alone prevailed without these other values. Each of these values is also easily perverted, if an effort is made to press it directly into the service of one of the others. This is particularly true of both thought and art, which quickly degenerate into propaganda if moral considerations become too overriding, and it can be easily true of religion as well.

The role of formal religion, of the Church in society, is relatively easy to define in these terms. Personal sensibilities, while the individual is perhaps born with them, must also be cultivated, and a child who grows up amid routine ugliness and receives a philistine education is unlikely to appreciate beauty on any deep level. Religious sensibilities must also be systematically cultivated, and part of the apparent insularity and hypocrisy of the churches in America is perhaps due to their faltering attempts to cultivate sensibilities which the larger culture unwittingly seeks to blunt and destroy. (Artists too are inclined to gather in ghettoes and colonies.) Francis Carling, although generally unsympathetic to Catholic education, says that "continual awareness of the spiritual requires constant practice; the soul needs exercise. The regular practice of religion by Catholic youngsters, when it is more than a habitual reflex, has the effect of creating and maintaining a world of the spirit that might otherwise go unperceived . . . the emphasis on worship in our early training had the great advantage of creating a strong sense of the spiritual." [30]

The Church is important therefore because it is the only institution, the only community, which systematically seeks to inculcate, disseminate, meditate upon, and publicly affirm values having to do specifically with God and transcendence. (Other communities divorced from the Church might conceivably do the same, but most of these communities seem to repudiate, or to drift away from, any concern with transcendence.) The Church must always attempt, strenuously, to relate its belief in transcendence to the needs of the society around it, but this striving after relevance can never be at the price of the Church's central insights into transcendence. There are many groups and many individuals in society willing to provide strong moral witness and social commitment; the Church alone can provide hints of eternity.

Traditional Christians tended to convict non-believers of moral failure, of some kind of personal moral flaw which inhibited belief in God. Non-belief should perhaps rather be seen as failure of the imagination, which is never morally reprehensible. Harvey Cox, having celebrated secularity in the mid 1960's, came by the end of that decade to celebrate fantasy, and predictably there were many Catholic radicals who followed him without missing a step. (The secularizers of 1965 urged Christians to rid themselves of their archaic and irrelevant concern with worship, mystery, and transcendence. Many of these same individuals by 1970 were castigating these same Christians for stodginess and lack of imagination. Whatever mainstream Christians may do, in the eyes of the radicals it will never be right.) Knowledge of God is exceedingly difficult in modern Western culture, but the difficulties do not excuse Christians from trying. Too many radicals seem to have opted for the easy alternative of defining as "God" everything in the world which seems humanly meaningful and satisfying. This procedure cannot help but seem rather dishonest and presumptuous to many non-believers, who would probably prefer to enjoy human satisfactions in their own terms, without being told that unknown to themselves they have been encountering God. (In some ways this formulation is even more arrogant and patronizing than the old exclusivism.) It is also a way by which the troubled radical can dispose of the problem of God easily and without cost, a way of avoiding the hard spiritual and imaginative struggles which would be necessary to make God real and personal.

Numerous religious and laymen, for whom God was real and love of God a conscious motivating force prior to the reform, have since found that secularity, and only secularity, now defines their horizon. James Langford, a lay editor, describes in his own life a situation which has been experienced by many individuals in the past decade. Once, he relates, God was real to him, love of God was a call to both contemplation and action, and death itself had meaning. Now, however, theology "is attempting to catch up with the world," and he has left his "shelter . . . those moments when God seemed so real, so easy to contact. I have gone out into the world where Diogenes and Nietzsche, Sartre and Bernanos live. . . . Is it too bland to say that simply to hope, to be open to life in a new way every moment, is itself the life of prayer?" [31] This seems a moving and honest expression of an archetypal and modern experience. But there is again the implied assumption that those who know God in a special way do not really know anything, that the loss of such awareness is really no loss, that the agnosticism of modern, secular Western man is somehow normative and must be embraced by every honest individual. Why should the world of Diogenes, Nietzsche, Sartre, and Bernanos be a more real place than the world of Paul or Francis of Assisi, Luther or Kierkegaard, Marcel or John XXIII? A religious reform which ends in man's inability to know God except in vague traces may simply be a reform which has failed. Reformers cannot, however, allow themselves to consider this a real possibility.

Whatever its many and obvious failings, the great achievement of the Catholic Church has been to keep alive in the souls of many, many individuals a sense that God is real and loves them in a personal way. This is an achievement of extreme importance, and yet it is the achievement which radicals and many reformers dismiss entirely and refuse even to look at. In the midst of a culture officially hospitable to such a belief, but in fact dedicated to undermining it in every possible way by teaching men to trust their own infinite manipulative abilities, it is not possible to achieve this awareness except by a certain attachment to tradition and a certain inwardness, a sense of the partial separation of the community of believers from the larger society. A sense of the past is necessary because in a society which offers men few traces of the divine the solidity of the past helps provide alternative modes of awareness and gives a certain measure of plausibility to implausible beliefs. The sociologists John B. Orr and F. Patrick Nichelson have suggested that "Catholicism is in great need of a theology of permanence, a reflective legitimation of its most beautiful resources. . . . Catholic progressives find themselves in the sad state of most white revolutionaries. They have little to bind themselves together except a common hatred of their past." [32]

Many progressives overlook the fact that the world is composed of an infinity of groups enjoying special identities; it is not a melting pot of homogeneously liberated secular men. As Daniel Callahan has suggested, some liberals see a progression towards a more open kind of religion, when in reality the necessary choice may be for or against religion.[33] Consciously or otherwise, most radicals seem already to have chosen against.

Progressives are fully justified in stressing the possibilities for men to encounter God in the world, through other men and through history. The Church is not the exclusive vehicle for knowledge of God. Yet it seems also evident that the knowledge of God found in the world is quite fragmentary and elusive. Those who have been raised as Christians and have had their religious sensibilities formed by the Church see many things in the world which they recognize as signs of God. Secularists who were not raised in a religious tradition do not usually interpret these same realities in the same way; they regard them as wholly natural and not as manifestations of God or the Spirit. The probable implication of this fact is that the abandonment of the Church and of religious education will insure that in future ages very few people will recognize any sign of God, either in traditional religion or in "the world." The sensibilities for this knowledge are being systematically neglected and allowed to atrophy.

The Church is, among other things, a collection and an intensification of those perceptions of God which men have had over the centuries. There are, inevitably, important omissions from this collection, and it is one of the reformer's tasks to assimilate some of these omissions, as for example the practice of Zen. On the whole, however, the Church presents to men such an array of spiritual styles, such accumulated religious experience, so many models of sainthood, that only arrogance can justify its dismissal as "irrelevant." God can be found in the world, and sometimes perhaps in a very profound way. But in general the Church has gathered and intensified the experiences of God and has made available to men methods, disciplines, and maps for living these experiences themselves. (Some of the methods have of course been unhelpful or worse, and are well discarded.) Nowhere will the sincere seeker find more ready access to God than through the Church, if he really looks.

Talk about the self-preoccupation, or ghettoization, of the Church is thus misleading, since the Church must always have a considerable (although not sole) preoccupation with its awareness of the divine, which to an outsider (including many outsiders who are nominally insiders) will seem to be self-absorption. In an inhospitable culture it is also necessary for the Church to exaggerate certain of its traits in order to emphasize the radical strangeness of its message and to guard against the easy assimilation which is modern society's most effective weapon against what is radical and strange. (Radicals who reject this notion in religion usually see its point in politics, where the radical young perceive the need to wear special clothes, use a special language, develop distinctive symbols, and live in ghettoes, precisely because of their realistic fear of being "co-opted" and their desire to impress on the jaded bourgeoisie precisely how radical their values are. In advanced religious circles it is now permissible to wear a peace medal but not a crucifix, a dashiki or an Indian headband but not a cassock, and it is permissible to chant Buddhist prayers ritualistically but not to use Latin or say the rosary. There is no talk about ghettoization or exhortations to universal identity when the radical really believes in a particular cause.)

The great religious ideal of contemplation teaches that knowledge of God is ultimately a value in itself, without reference to practical action in the world. The Church needs both action and contemplation, and the radical program now, indeed much of the post-conciliar reform, seems bent on eliminating contemplation from the lives of Christians, forcing them to equate their Christianity with worldly involvement. Ultimately, there should be no apology for the religious sense, as there should be no apology for the artistic sense. The Eucharist may serve as the basis for a communal gathering, but that is scarcely its primary function and certainly does not exhaust its meaning. Confession may be a form of therapy, but its significance does not depend on that. Unless Catholics are able to perceive the core, specifically religious meaning of their mysteries, the mysteries will quickly lose all meaning, as they have already done for many people. The liturgy, and Christian doctrines, are now undergoing the same fate art undergoes when it is pressed into the service of politics or morals—it cheapens and loses its power.

The Church's greatest disservice to the world would be at present to abandon its sense of God and transcendence, its accumulated spirituality, to join the world in its perplexed secularity. If the apparent stirrings toward a renewed spirituality among the young have any authenticity, the Church has immense resources to give towards this end. Once the living, continuous sense of the divine and of the spirit are lost (at present they are already highly attenuated), it will be immeasurably more difficult to recover them in the future. This is one important function of tradition in the Church—to preserve resources which may, at some time to someone, prove valuable. This, however, also requires that the tradition of the Church be a living one, which radicals are studiously attempting to undermine.

Many radicals, while conceding that the Church has kept alive a sense of the divine among men, also think that the quality of this awareness has been such as to vitiate the achievement. In particular the popular devotions of the Church have come under severe attack since the conciliar years. In some parishes they have simply been suppressed, by order of the priests. Some progressive clergy have conceived a special mission for themselves in ridiculing and otherwise discrediting popular piety. School children in most places are given no introduction to the great array of saints, novenas, and so on which used to form the mainstream of popular devotion.

There is a great deal of dishonesty and bad faith here, however. If popular piety has often been shallow, sentimental, and superstitious, it has also been genuinely popular. Its origins have often been with the people, with the laity, and reformers who talk about the "people of God" but despise popular devotions are simply being hypocritical. The progressive intellectual is often charmed and touched by folk culture when he encounters it in an exotic setting, and he can rail eloquently against the Western missionaries' impulse to suppress native customs. But he has no use for folk culture when it exists in his own tradition, and he is continuously trying to rid himself of all its traces. Popular Catholic culture is now in a situation comparable to peasant culture at the time of the Industrial Revolution—it is being rapidly eroded and assimilated by a subtly anti-religious modernity; forthright advocates of modernity regard it as unspeakably narrow and backward and hasten its death; when the triumph of modernity is complete, future intellectuals will realize that something precious has been lost and will try vainly to recover elements of the suppressed culture.

For all its obvious failures, popular Catholic piety fulfilled the one indispensable purpose of religion—it gave to millions of people a lively sense of God. Reformers who attacked this piety were often quite ignorant of it. William DuBay, for example, says that "Catholics pray often and poorly. They rarely speak of their own needs, which is how prayer should begin." [34] Yet the public expressions of popular devotion suggest that if anything its principal weakness was its overemphasis on personal needs, an exclusive concentration on petitionary prayer. Father Gerard Sloyan seems already to have forgotten the very existence of popular piety. The pastor who is not formed by modern liturgical theories, he says, will by default be forced to preach on anti-Communism, women's dress, hyper-patriotism, or "the Church as partisan allegiance." [35] The vast collection of traditional devotions are here quietly pushed from sight, as though they did not exist.

Reformers were often acute in their criticisms of popular devotions, but they overlooked a simple fact—they really had nothing with which to replace them. Popular piety had withstood religion's most severe test—it had proven itself able to penetrate deeply into men's souls, to form their sensibilities, to give expression to their sense of mystery and their religious strivings. There is nothing comparable in the reformed Church. Those who have taken away the rosaries, the vigil lights, the statues, and the novenas appear to have not the slightest clue as to how to kindle the same depth of feeling, the same religious awareness, in the masses. (It is well to recall that originally the attack on popular piety was made in the name of the Mass. The Eucharistic Sacrifice and the Real Presence were said by reformers to be so fundamental to the faith that such items as devotion to the saints were an intolerable distraction. Later many of these same reformers quietly dropped their own strong belief in the Mass and effectively denied the Eucharistic Sacrifice and the Real Presence.)

The demise of popular piety is itself part of a larger development in the Church which is perhaps the most significant aspect of *aggiornamento,* although it has rarely been noticed—the disappearance of all symbolism unique to Catholic life. Catholicism has always been a religion of symbol; it is this above all which gives it its affinity with Eastern Orthodoxy and certain kinds of Anglicanism, and sets it off from classic Protestantism. When conservatives speak of the "Protestantizing" of the Church they may be thinking of specifics like new doctrines concerning the sacraments and the priesthood, or the weakening of papal and episcopal authority. The most significant Protestantizing, however, has been the quiet suppression of almost all specifically Catholic symbolism. Contrary to general belief, Catholicism has never taught that man can reach God only through the mediation of the priest. This is true of the official piety—the sacraments. But the unofficial, popular piety, which has always been far more influential than the official piety, has never required a priest. What Catholicism has instead generally taught is that man can attain God only through symbols. Radical Catholicism, insofar as it concerns itself with God at all, is Protestant in its implicit denial of the efficacy of religious symbols. Most traditional symbols have simply been suppressed. (Advanced liturgies are now commonly celebrated in rooms bare of all statues and crucifixes, decorated only with posters proclaiming humanistic slogans.) Those symbols which have been retained are often transmuted to give them a "universal," humanistic meaning (such as the Mass as community meal, confession as community reconciliation, the Resurrection as man's willingness to change his life). This radicalism often becomes a rather fanatic puritanism, in which traditional customs and traditional symbols are ruthlessly hacked away as "meaningless" or "superstitious" and the physical aspects of worship are regarded as totally unimportant. (Thus some radical priests no longer wear vestments at the Eucharist. Catholics are urged to cease building churches and to begin holding services in living rooms, storefronts, meeting halls. Rich traditional gestures like the sign of the cross, genuflecting, prostration, are reduced to utilitarian sitting, standing and handshaking. The extravagance of incense, flowers, and banks of candles is banished for the sake of chaste austerity.)

This puritanism is quiet puzzling among people who profess their desire to be worldly and who also wish to embrace man's physical nature without inhibition or embarrassment. It is further evidence that the "worldliness" of most radicals is a very cerebral thing. They are in reality scandalized not only at the discovery of widespread sin among their fellow Christians, but also at the fact that so many men appear to have an "unclean" religious belief which depends on symbols and other physical expressions. Before the Council there was an exciting renaissance of religious art, as modern churches and modern renderings of traditional themes caught the imagination of many people. Since the Council, however, religious art as such has all but disappeared. (This dislike of the physical among radicals manifests itself in other ways also—their belief that the resurrection of the body, either of Christ or of other human beings, is unimportant to Christianity and probably untrue, and their distaste for the idea that Christ is physically present in the Eucharist.)

The disappearance or subtle discrediting of traditional religious symbolism is perhaps the primary cause of the deep religious malaise which now seems to affect so many Catholics. Men are not angels, and it is misguided fanaticism to decree that the concrete symbols, which for so many people have sustained a living interest in God, should be suppressed. Symbols have formed and mediated Catholics' religious sensibilities, and the sudden disappearance of so many of these symbols has caused a precipitous decline of faith among many. (The inability of so many people to experience any sense of the supernatural, for example, is probably related closely to styles of church music. Gregorian chant and Palestrina gave expression and form to a sensibility which the newer music excludes.)

In 1970 a lay group in Boston polled over 19,000 Catholics in that archdiocese concerning their preferences for a future archbishop. A heavy majority favored some lay voice in his selection, a limited term of office, and annual public reports on archdiocesan affairs. Obviously, these were not conservatives in the ordinary sense. (About 55 per cent said they wanted a moderate as archbishop, and 32 per cent a liberal.) Yet 71 per cent rejected having a "social activist" or an "administrator" as archbishop in favor of a "spiritual leader." [36] Obviously, despite the claim of many radicals that "spirituality" is a trivial chimera and that action in the world should distinguish the modern Catholic, this category has meaning for many laymen, who are looking to the Church for spiritual leadership.

The greatest failure of the pre-conciliar Church was its lack of adequate spiritual guidance, even for members of religious orders. It is a failure which reformers have, if anything, compounded by their repudiation of the old forms of piety without any adequate newer resources. (It is intolerable, for example, that the creation of new liturgies should often be in the hands of those who have nothing but dislike for the old liturgies. Their lack of any tradition or foundation has often led to bizarre and rootless improvisations. Most radicals are unable to distinguish nostalgia and blind reaction from living tradition.) The writings of radical theologians, although sometimes informed by passion, are almost devoid of any apparent living contact with God or Christ. In this respect they are certainly no advance over the dry Scholasticism of the old manuals.

What is more frightening even than the apparent absence of living spirituality in so many progressives is their lack of interest in the very subject, and their neglect of the entire Christian spiritual heritage between the Bible and Vatican II. A generation of clergy and other religious leaders are apparently being educated with scarcely any regard for spirituality as it has been understood, and without even any contacts with the spiritual heritage of the Church, or any belief that it is significant. (Indeed, in some radical circles its very existence is denied—the history of the Church is officially regarded as a desert before Vatican II.) The flurries of renewed interest in prayer, mysticism, and religious symbolism seem to have come primarily from persons outside the Church, not from radicals within. Among some radicals there is a hostility to everything connected with spirituality. Thus the literary critic Doris Grumbach proposes a nine-point plan for making "useful" the cathedral of Albany (N.Y.), which is situated in the center of the business district. Her nine suggestions involve worthy proposals for feeding the poor, providing space for militant groups, and so forth.[37] But there is no suggestion that a space in the center of the city reserved for prayer and recollection may have some value. Catholic radicals are in certain ways in revolt against their society, but they often show themselves to be deeply infected with American pragmatism. No doctrine, no religious practice, no building which is not "useful" is to them justified. American society fears silence and fears emptiness, both of which cannot help appearing wasteful. Among traditional religion's strongest resources are precisely its ability to create and to validate occasions for silence, contemplation, emptiness in the sense of cessation from activity and worldly meaning. Radical Christians now appear often to abhor these occasions. An empty church standing in the midst of a busy city is a radical judgment on that city, a continuous call to man to pause occasionally to look into himself, and remember God. "Updated" churches, however, seem to be designed to discourage private prayer. There are often no kneelers, and the seats are hard benches without back rests. The retreat move-

210

ment too has apparently concluded that even a few days' silence in a year is too much for contemporary man, and retreats are now organized as discussion groups around matters of secular concern.

Not only reactionaries have been concerned over ill-conceived changes. A few years before his death Thomas Merton wrote that "one fears that in the reforms and renovation that are now under way there may be no end of hasty, ill-considered and sweeping changes in which a lot that is profoundly significant and alive will be discarded thoughtlessly." [38] Among the many evidences that Father Merton's predictions have come true is the fact that so many Catholics now feel there is no necessity even to attempt to pray, see no point at all in the contemplative life, and believe that a living awareness of God and Christ are rather unimportant.

Naturally, the most important focus of spirituality, for Catholics, is the liturgy, and it is in the area of liturgical reform that the most significant successes and failures have occurred. It is also the area in which the reformers' self-willed isolation from the mass of believers has been most evident.

In general radicals, and many progressives, regard the old liturgy much as they regard the old popular piety—disdainfully, as a collection of archaic, superstitious, and irrelevant practices in need of severe purification and restructuring by experts. Most liturgical reformers, however, if they ever understood the actual workings of the old liturgy, do not understand them now. They overlook the fact that this alleged religious desert attracted larger numbers of persons to voluntary daily observances than do the newer rites, a fact which can be explained only by assuming that pious laymen are mindless fools. The solemn celebra-

tions of the greater feasts seem to have raised religious sensibilities to heights never attained in the newer liturgies. What the
liturgist assumes to have been a boring, meaningless experience
was often quite meaningful to many people, because they did
not so much take meaning from it as bring meaning to it. They
believed that something of infinite importance was happening at
the altar, and hence to them the experience was not empty. The
Latin, and the priest's silence, also forced many people to interiorize both their devotions and their understanding of the
Eucharist, and if this was perhaps not the ideal form of participation at Mass it was nonetheless a religious exercise which few
people now have occasion to go through and it probably accounts for the serene faith which is often encountered in life-
long daily communicants. Those who think that the old liturgy
was irrelevant to life overlook the experience once attainable in
large downtown churches, in which persons of the most diverse
social classes—impoverished old ladies, policemen on the beat,
students, prosperous businessmen, factory laborers—gathered
spontaneously for a brief time before returning once more to the
world. There was even an unrecognized kind of community
here—even if they did not greet each other they shared a common sense of what was happening in the liturgy, and why they
were there. As John B. Orr and F. Patrick Nichelsen observe,
"Instead of using principle to separate angelic man from creation, Catholicism offers pervasive rationalization of all styles of
living. Behind an ordered worship and preaching there is an
almost mystical confidence in the chaotic universe: Just break
bread together and then go, separately, and do your own
thing. . . ."[39]

Perhaps the most fundamental failure of the reforming liturgists is their failure even to understand what they think liturgy is, or what it should do. If on one level this is honest confusion mirroring the times, on another it is also arrogance—the reforming liturgist often puts himself beyond criticism simply because there are no acknowledged standards by which his work can be judged. In the Liturgical Conference, for example, the basic conceptions of liturgy and its functions have changed numerous times in ten years.

The new liturgy, whether by design or by accident, seems especially ineffective in conveying to worshippers a sense of transcendence and deep spirituality. Prayers and readings have a straightforward and matter-of-fact quality devoid of deep reverberations or memorable rhythms. Progressive clergy tend to preach almost exclusively on matters pertaining to worldly living or communal identities. There is often a wearying over-emphasis on "love," "person," "creativity," "openness," and so on. There are few striking or dramatic gestures, symbols, or actions. When it is successful the new liturgy is a gathering of sincere, enlightened individuals engaged in a rather vague communal expression of their rather vague religious beliefs. The reformed liturgy rarely seems to point to anything much beyond itself.

Among reformers this failure to point towards transcendence is perhaps unintentional, although it seems also to reflect a certain insensitivity to transcendent values. Among radicals, however, it is a deliberate policy, dictated by the underlying dogmatic assumption that religion and social involvement are antithetical to each other. Radicals seem distressed at the idea that Catholics might spend as much as one hour a week consciously recalling

God and attempting to focus their thoughts on him; they are determined that this hour too shall be forcibly related to worldly concerns. James Colainni, expressing a doctrine which later seems to have become official in the Liturgical Conference, insisted that " 'Worship' is a word religion should try to forget." [40] As Louis Dupré pointed out, a syncretic liturgy incorporating elements of non-Christian worship and totally secular elements may be momentarily exciting, but such things usually signal the end of a religious era.[41] The radicals' attempts to secularize liturgy show far better than any polemic that liturgy is for them spiritually dead.

The Lutheran pastor Richard John Neuhaus, who considers himself a radical, notes that radical liturgies are usually now organized around small, homogeneous groups which emphasize spontaneity and appropriate the music and values of the youth culture. The emphasis is on "celebrating" reality, which is sometimes indistinguishable from adjusting to it. The minds to which it addresses itself are found on a rather narrow span of the political spectrum—from left-liberal to revolutionary. This liturgy develops primarily by attaching itself to whatever seems currently fashionable in radical secular circles. Pastor Neuhaus doubts if this is really the effective liturgy of the future and points to the radicals' tendency to dissolve liturgy into life and politics, as though there were no specific human activity which could be called liturgy.[42]

Probably no aspect of renewal has been so troubling to radicals as the problem of liturgy, which like so many of their problems has been a self-created one wholly incapable of solution within the framework of their assumptions. Traditional liturgy was always understood to be the worship of God, although it also served other purposes. (The meaning in apparently meaningless liturgies came from the worshippers' conviction that they were really addressing God.) Having decided that worship of God is not the purpose of liturgy (worship appears to have no practical value, hence is a meaningless activity), radicals must search desperately to find a justification for an activity whose fundamental meaning has been vacated. Inevitably, they encounter the problem pointed out by Louis Dupré—symbols cannot be arbitrarily given new meanings; old forms cannot be arbitrarily appropriated to new functions, except by geniuses. In attempting to justify liturgy in wholly human terms—as empathy, as community, as celebration—they allow themselves no real way of distinguishing liturgy from life. There is no worldly function which liturgy serves which cannot be served better through other means. Empathy is better developed in sensitivity training. Community is better encountered at parties and small dinners. Social concern is better stimulated by polemics or the experience of injustice. Celebration is something people best do spontaneously, without reference to an ordained structure. Many radicals have finally concluded that liturgy itself has no meaning for them; others will probably reach this same conclusion in time; much radical liturgical experiment appears merely to be staving off that inevitable day. (John D. Groppe, an English professor, describes an "experiment in exposure education," which he regards as a valid new form of liturgy. It consists of "rap sessions," sensitivity encounters, visits to bars and peep shows, lectures on North American oppression of Latin America, movies, and a rock dance band. As Richard Neuhaus has said with respect to other liturgical experiments, "Something which is everything is for all practical purposes nothing." [43])

Perhaps the last gasp of liturgical experimentation, like the last gasp of civilization itself, is the pursuit of experience without reference to the quality of the experience, or its meaning. The Jesuit liturgist C. J. McNaspy described the 1969 Liturgical Week thus: "This sense of a contrived, artificially induced experience obscured any sense of genuine celebration, at least for a great many." It was, he said, "shooting from the hip by earnest cowboys who haven't got a theological clue,[44]" and this is an experience not difficult to duplicate among the numerous attempts at liturgical breakthroughs. (When Harvey Cox made "fantasy" and "celebration" respectable, there rose up liturgical pioneers possessed of the souls of recreation directors earnestly and grimly exhorting their flocks to have fun, hang loose, celebrate, and fantasize. Some literal-minded liturgical reformers apparently believe that people cannot possibly be at peace with each other unless they are forced to shake hands.)

The crucial problem of radical liturgical reform is its separation from the more fundamental problem of faith. Many Catholic radicals seem to be seeking a Christianity not requiring faith, and they have endeavored to keep liturgy alive without asking what meaning it can have once a lively sense of God has vanished. As is usually the case when coherent, stable values are uprooted, there is a desperate desire to substitute experiences and intense feelings and to keep these constantly burning. One of the self-created failures of radical liturgy and radical religion is its implied hope of discovering ways of maintaining a continuous sense of excitement and emotional stimulation among participants, which no movement can possibly achieve. The flagging of excitement and emotion is then inevitably taken as the failure of the new liturgy, or the new religion, and the radical is left even more jaded than before, desperately seeking for renewed stimulation, or else wearily despairing.

Traditional Catholicism was remarkably effective in sustaining a living sense of God in many people, but it was also highly effective in the alternative task—articulating religious meaning for people whose religious belief was rarely exciting or emotionally satisfying. Virtually all of the world's great spiritual masters—East and West—warn against the assumption that spiritual profundity can be equated with emotional intensity and emotional satisfaction. They rather advise the disciple to be wary of such experiences, which often distract from the central truths and which are never more than a preliminary to deeper discoveries. The "dark night of the soul," the feelings of aridity and emptiness, of separation from God, are themselves often a necessary stage in spiritual advancement. Religious radicals usually seem unaware of these teachings, or else unconcerned with them. In a society whose avant-garde makes being "turned on" the primary end of living, Catholics in touch with their tradition are in a favored position to offer alternatives, and to begin picking up the pieces once the god of experience again shows his clay feet. Radical Catholics, however, too often seem excited and mesmerized by the drug culture, the rock culture, the culture of total sensual fulfillment. Their vision of religious renewal appears to be simply that of assimilating religion to this counter-culture, usually in stumbling and amateurish ways.

Traditional spirituality effectively introduced men to a measured pace in the spiritual life, in which great excitement or heights of ecstasy were rarely attained but there was a steady warmth. There is probably more wisdom in these words of a Virginia housewife than in the speculations of most post-conciliar spiritual experts:

There have been other urgings for us, the day-in-day-out people, to let the Spirit fill us, whereupon we will be dancing, singing, leaping with joy. It sounds beautiful. I'd like to do all these things. . . . Do tell us how a middle-aged person with responsibilities to children and pets, with a job that is confining and burdensome 85 per cent of the time, with debts for the basic needs of life . . . who must deal in and out of the home with personality conflicts—do tell us how this person will behave in each case when he is filled with this glorious joy.

It is my belief that people who go on doing their job each day, grimly sometimes, but accepting, when there seems no reason for doing so, those who stay in the struggle when God seems far away and faith an empty word—these people also know that "The Spirit speaks to our Spirit." [45]

Radicals who aspire to be worldly do not seem to have much to say to such persons; their concept of worldliness usually takes little notice of these realities, with which traditional spirituality was quite familiar. Like theology itself, or spirituality itself, these kinds of human problems are often dismissed as privatistic, inward-turned, and egocentric, and the radicals' vision of man sometimes seems to be of the perfect activist who has no distracting private life. Traditional spirituality, besides its achievement in conveying a sense of God's presence (often an implicit, ingrained sense surviving all manner of emotional dryness), was also able to relate itself quite effectively to the great but routine crises of human existence—birth and death, triumph and sorrow, raising children and caring for old people. It immeasurably helped very many people to cope with illness and disappointment, loneliness and despair. It is because so many radicals lack a sense of life's givens that they dismiss this kind of piety. Revolutionary ideology requires the belief that all things can be changed for the better; in time the obdurancy of reality will again begin to assert itself, and the resources of traditional spirituality will again be respected. (Radicals often imply that all problems are political and can be alleviated by political action. But illness, personal loss, loneliness beset people of all social classes.)

Radicals have also been too hasty in dismissing traditional piety as irrelevant to their political concerns. Daniel Berrigan, on the contrary, makes specific comparison between the situation of his brother Philip, in solitary confinement for destroying draft files, and the Elizabethan Jesuits hiding in airless "priest holes." [46] The inherited ideal of sanctity is perhaps not as irrelevant as is often supposed. Further he relates how, on the night of Thomas Merton's death, he prayed to Merton to effect Philip's release from jail (an earlier imprisonment), and the release was effected.[47] Usually this kind of piety arouses feelings of anger, contempt, or pity in progressives, and they consider themselves infinitely above it. Daniel Berrigan himself has presented Catholics with an authentic contemporary model of sanctity, precisely because he fuses deep concern for man, and political involvement, with an apparently unshakable and basically simple faith in God. As with all saints, the model is ambiguous. (It is not entirely clear, for example, that his actions have been politically relevant, but it is not the business of saints to be relevant in this sense.) But Father Berrigan's actions suggest that for the Catholic a deep traditional piety may still be the most powerful motive for social concern. (Progressives are sometimes made uncomfortable by other manifestations of traditional sanctity, as for example by Maryknoll Bishop James E. Walsh, released in 1970 after eighteen years in a Chinese prison. Since they are convinced that the old piety was essentially pointless, they usually ignore these reminders of the heroism it was able to forge in some men.) There are numerous other possibilities for making traditional spirituality relevant, most of which progressives have neglected. The concept of mortal sin, for example, is a useful way of explaining a moral phenomenon like racism—a condition of the soul which transcends specific individual actions, which infects the entire soul and thus vitiates the good done in other ways, which can only be lifted through complete contrition. The popular canonizations of John F. Kennedy and Martin Luther King, complete with images reverently venerated in simple homes, demonstrates that traditional hagiography is far from dead.

The radical program, which at present seems informed by intensity and passion, paradoxically promises a future Church which will be bland and devoid of tension, since there will be no conceivable conflict between secular and religious values. (William DuBay warns against "the modern false prophets who speak about the tension that should exist between the world and the Church." [48]) But it is precisely in this tension that the most creative movements of historic Catholicism have always originated, and it is doubtful whether a religion freed of this tension, in which men no longer think of themselves as in some sense stretched between two worlds, will be able to generate true greatness. For all its failings, Catholicism has thus far avoided the utter blandness of some sects of Protestantism, because at least its priests and people have taken seriously certain quite strange and alien notions, certain mysteries which have repeatedly intruded themselves into their lives. Ivan Illich, the radical Latin American priest, says that "I make a scrupulous distinction between the church as She and the church as It. *She* is the surprise in the net, the pearl. She is the mystery, the kingdom among us. The identity of the Church as She will remain through whatever changes . . ." [49]

There is among most progressives no evident sense of their grappling, as Catholics, with a mystery which is at times horrifying and repulsive, at times sublime, but always larger than the self or the sociological categories which are now so nimbly flicked about. There is little of the puzzled acceptance of both the divine and the human which Graham Greene's characters achieve. It is here, ultimately, in their lack of concern for this mystery of the Church, that Catholic radicals fully reveal themselves as not Catholic at all and, in terms of the imagination and the infinite possibilities for human existence, not radical at all.

Notes

1. *St. Louis Review*, Aug. 14, 1970, p. 8.
2. Novak, *A New Generation* (New York, 1964), p. 157.
3. *Commonweal*, May 31, 1968, pp. 323-5; also quoted in *U.S. Catholic and Jubilee*, June, 1969, p. 10.
4. Colaianni, *The Catholic Left*, p. 117.
5. DuBay, *The Human Church*, pp. 13, 81, 94.
6. *Commonweal*, Sept. 4, 1970, p. 440.
7. *Ibid.*, Aug. 19, 1966, pp. 530-3.
8. *Ibid.*, May 31, 1968, p. 329.
9. *Ibid.*, Dec. 29, 1967, p. 406.
10. *Ibid.*, Oct. 31, 1969, pp. 128-9.

11. *Ibid.*, March 6, 1970, p. 613.

12. *Ibid.*, March 20, 1970, p. 47.

13. *Ibid.*, Aug. 22, 1969, pp. 514-5.

14. *Worship*, Aug.-Sept., 1968, p. 414.

15. *Spiritual Life*, Spring, 1970, pp. 74-9.

16. *National Catholic Reporter*, Aug. 7, 1970, p. 7.

17. *Saturday Evening Post*, Dec. 28, 1968, p. 67.

18. *The Critic*, Oct.-Nov., 1967, p. 23.

19. *National Catholic Reporter*, May 22, 1970, pp. 10-11; *St. Louis Review*, June 26, 1970, p. 11.

20. *Commonweal*, April 28, 1967, p. 174.

21. *Ibid.*, Oct. 31, 1969, p. 157.

22. *Spiritual Life*, Summer, 1970, pp. 126-7.

23. Quoted by Malcolm Muggeridge, *Esquire*, Oct., 1969, p. 44.

24. *National Catholic Reporter*, July 10, 1970, p. 12.

25. *Ibid.*, Aug. 7, 1970, p. 7.

26. *St. Louis Post-Dispatch*, Aug. 20, 1970, p. 6B.

27. *Commonweal*, March 27, 1970, p. 60.

28. *The Christian Century*, July 8, 1970, p. 842.

29. *Commonweal*, Nov. 5, 1965, p. 166.

30. Carling, *Move Over!*, pp. 91-2.

31. *Spiritual Life*, Summer, 1970, pp. 132-4.

32. Quoted by Andrew Greeley, *National Catholic Reporter*, Aug. 21, 1970, p. 13.

33. Donald Cutler (ed.), *The Religious Situation, 1968* (Boston, 1968), p. 239.

34. DuBay, *The Human Church*, p. 116.

35. *Commonweal*, March 27, 1970, p. 59.

36. *National Catholic Reporter*, July 10, 1970, p. 6.

37. *Commonweal*, May 30, 1969, pp. 316-7.

38. *Ibid.*, Feb. 7, 1964, p. 574.

39. Quoted by Andrew Greeley, *National Catholic Reporter*, Aug. 21, 1970, p. 13.

40. Colaianni, *The Catholic Left*, pp. 26-7.

41. *National Catholic Reporter*, June 19, 1970, p. 10.

42. *Commonweal*, Oct. 31, 1969, pp. 129-34.

43. *Ibid.*, p. 132.

44. *America,* Oct. 18, 1969, pp. 321-2.

45. *National Catholic Reporter,* June 5, 1970, p. 7.

46. *Commonweal,* Aug. 7, 1970, p. 384.

47. Reported by Francine du Plessix Gray, *National Catholic Reporter,* Aug. 21, 1970, p. 12.

48. DuBay, *The Human Church,* p. 47.

49. Reported by Francine Gray, *The New Yorker,* April 25, 1970, p. 80.

Appendix

Twenty-Six Heretical Notions Characterizing Radical Catholicism

(1) Human opinions and human actions are wholly determined by history, and it is therefore futile for men to resist the movement of history. What appears as "unprogressive" cannot therefore be regarded as the authentic movement of history but merely its apparent movement.

(2) Traditions consequently have no value, except insofar as they can be appropriated to the use of "progressive" movements.

(3) The major contours of the future can be known by at least a few enlightened individuals, and all men have a moral obligation to work towards this perceived future.

(4) Men of the emerging future will be possessed of total freedom and spontaneity and will have no need for laws, customs, traditions, and institutions.

(5) Humanity is evolving into a higher state of being in which the moral and intellectual limitations which have always characterized the species will disappear.

(6) Part of this evolution is the convergence to a universal consciousness on the part of all sorts and conditions of men. Special identities such as race, nation, and religion will disappear. Those who affirm special identities are therefore acting against history and against the Spirit. An exception are those

separatist movements which appear to be progressive, such as Black Power.

(7) All special religious identities are consequently a form of infidelity to the Gospel. Nothing of any consequence separates Catholics and Protestants, Christians and non-Christians, believers and non-believers.

(8) All meaningful human experiences manifest God, and thus particular "religious" experiences are unnecessary and pointless.

(9) Whatever appears to be enlightened, idealistic, and future-oriented is "the world." All else is really not of the world.

(10) One of the principal obligations of Christians is to harmonize their beliefs and their lives with this emerging world. Failure to do so is infidelity to the Spirit and to the Gospel.

(11) To be fully "human" is equivalently moral perfection; sin is inhuman and resides chiefly in institutions and social customs.

(12) Men have vitually limitless powers of creation, so that the destruction or abandonment of everything inherited from the past will be followed by an adequate reconstruction of all necessary values and patterns of living.

(13) Change is to be presumed good except in rare instances. Those who lack enthusiasm for change act contrary to both the Gospel and humanity. No man may validly choose to conserve old values and institutions.

(14) Authority in the Church is presently lodged with small groups of morally and intellectually enlightened persons who are not accountable to the masses or to the hierarchy. Such groups enjoy the guidance of the Spirit in a special way.

(15) The inspiration of the Spirit can be discerned in a variety of religious, political, and cultural movements which appear to

be progressive. Failure to join in these movements is consequently a form of infidelity.

(16) Man is incapable of discovering any form of valid meaning except in the human community, and aspirations towards transcendence are generally illusory and unhealthy.

(17) The Church is to be regarded wholly as a natural reality, to be understood in purely sociological terms. All religious beliefs can be explained similarly, and need not be respected once their social matrix has been revealed.

(18) Religious beliefs have meaning insofar as they can be translated into wholly human terms; otherwise they are meaningless and distracting.

(19) The Church is primarily a political reality, whose value is determined to the degree that it promotes social change and progress.

(20) Action in the world is therefore the principal vocation of the Christian, and contemplation and the spiritual life are at best accessories to this. Salvation, if such is possible, is achieved through politics.

(21) To be a true Christian a man must therefore be politically involved, in a "progressive" way.

(22) It is possible to be a Christian without interest in prayer or the spiritual life or God. The validity of these interests is at best problematical.

(23) Since the Christian's vocation is political, it is possible for him to harmonize his beliefs wholly with "the world," understood as the sum of all progressive realities. All emphasis on the Christian's estrangement from the world must be rejected.

(24) "Religion," as commonly understood, is essentially valueless and generally pernicious. This is especially true of popular

227

religion in the Catholic Church. Concern with "the supernatural" is a neurotic illusion.

(25) After centuries of obscurity, the true meaning of the Gospel is now being discovered by progressives. With rare exceptions, the Church has been unfaithful to the Gospel for at least 1600 years. The Protestant churches, although initially their influence was healthy, have been similarly corrupted through most of their history.

(26) Since about 1960 certain men have been experiencing a miraculous breakthrough in understanding of the Gospel, the nature of man and human society, and the shape of the future, which dwarfs anything since the days of the New Testament.